PAST & PRESENT

CAPITOL HILL

Opposite: In 1846, James Crutchett, a pioneer in the natural gas industry, bought this house at North Capitol and C Streets NE, built a gas plant on the property, and lit his house and outdoor lamps with gas, attracting wide attention, including from Congress. In 1847, he was contracted to light the Capitol and grounds with gas. His house, photographed between 1920 and 1929, was demolished around 1929 for the Senate Fountain. (Courtesy Historical Society of Washington, DC, CHS-05471.)

PAST & PRESENT

CAPITOL HILL

Elizabeth Purcell

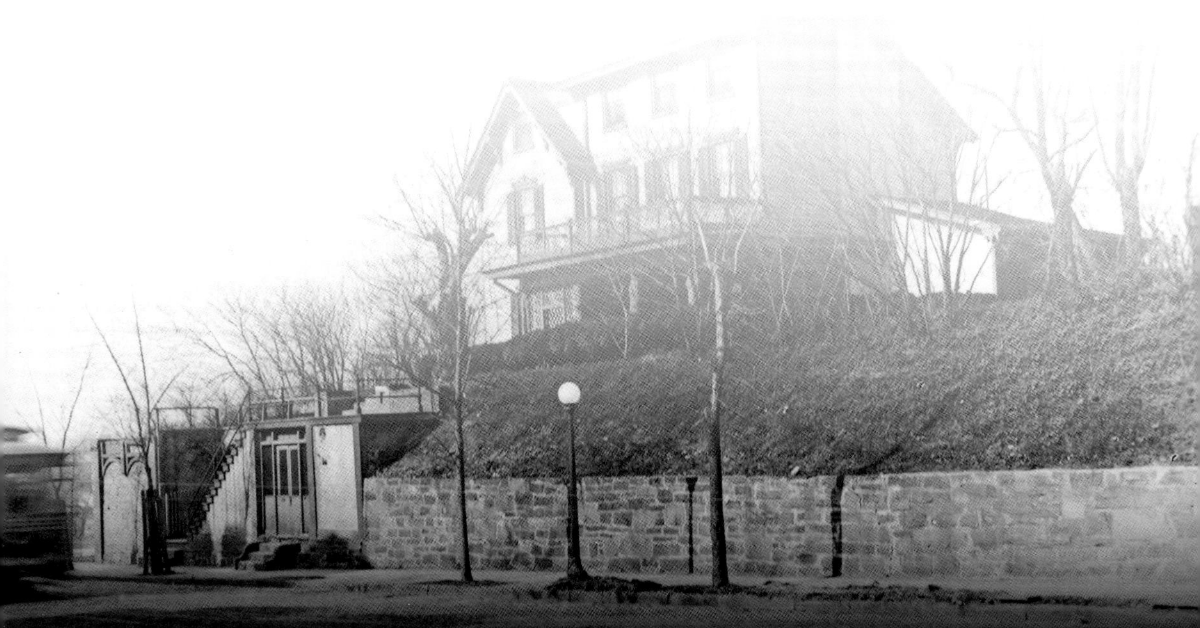

To Brian S. O'Grady.

ISBN 978-1-4671-0582-8

Library of Congress Control Number: 2020939817

Published by Arcadia Publishing
Charleston, South Carolina

Printed in the United States of America

For all general information, please contact Arcadia Publishing:
Telephone 843-853-2070
Fax 843-853-0044
E-mail sales@arcadiapublishing.com
For customer service and orders:
Toll-Free 1-888-313-2665

Visit us on the Internet at www.arcadiapublishing.com

On the Front Cover: Martin S. Fealy (1875–1940) operated his drugstore at 1024 Pennsylvania Avenue SE between approximately 1905 and 1938. It is shown in a photograph taken between 1910 and 1935. Streetcar tracks ran through the median. By 1948, Fealy's Drugstore was gone, replaced by a service station, which was replaced in turn by the Butterfield House condominiums in 2008. The round tower of 420 Tenth Street is visible in the background of both photographs. (Past image courtesy Library of Congress Prints & Photographs Division, LC-F82-7; present image author's collection.)

On the Back Cover: Elizabeth A. Haines, a widow, first operated a successful dry goods store near the Navy Yard. In 1892, needing more space, she hired Julius Germuiller to design a three-story brick building at 801 Pennsylvania Avenue SE. The store offered 50 departments on two stories, plus third-story offices. After she sold the building in 1911, another department store and several furniture stores used the building, including Nachman's, seen in the past photograph from 1910 to 1935. (Courtesy Library of Congress Prints & Photographs Division, LC-F8314-18005X.)

CONTENTS

ACKNOWLEDGMENTS

I wish to thank Nancy Metzger for her wisdom and generous advice. I am very grateful for the following people: Stephen Morris for his help; Kathleen Crabb, DC Department of Transportation librarian; Anne McDonough and Jessica Smith, the Historical Society of Washington, DC; Kimberly E. Springle and Crystal L. Hurd, Sumner School Museum; Leslie Matthaei, Architect of the Capitol; Jerry McCoy, Washingtoniana Division, DC Public Library; Melissa Lindberg, Library of Congress Prints & Photographs Division (LOC); Brian D. Kraft for advice on maps; Monte Edwards on the history of Washington Gas Light Company; Jim Thackaberry for advice on modern Capitol Hill buildings; and Neatha S. Sanders and Rudolph Westray on the history of Garfield Park. I also wish to thank my editors Caroline Anderson and Jim Kempert for their patience and advice.

Unless otherwise noted, all present-day photographs were taken by the author. Courtesy lines following each caption credit the source of the historical image.

Introduction

While most people think of Capitol Hill as only the US Capitol and the hill upon which it stands, Washington residents know that the neighborhood of Capitol Hill extends about 20 blocks east of the Capitol. This book explores buildings on Capitol Hill from the 1790s to 2020—where buildings were sited and why, and whether they survived or were replaced and why.

Congress scheduled moving the capital from Philadelphia to Washington for 1800 and expected to find on arrival completed public buildings including the Capitol and places to stay while Congress was meeting. Congress would pay only for moving expenses and not to construct public buildings. George Washington had persuaded the original landowners to contribute half of their land to the federal government and retain the other half, which presumably would greatly increase in value. The city was surveyed into squares and lots. Proceeds from the sale of government-owned lots would be a primary funding source for constructing public buildings. Lot purchasers were expected to make payments on land contracts and, in some cases, to construct buildings on their lots. This financing scheme attracted speculators such as James Greenleaf, who contracted to buy thousands of lots, then defaulted on payments, and tried to block reselling the lots. The resulting litigation lasted decades.

Beginning in the 1790s and continuing throughout the 19th century, residents, investors, and businesses constructed buildings for their needs, including houses, hotels, and stores. Many of these early buildings were clustered around the Capitol. However, this neighborhood was also the logical place for Congress to expand. Many early buildings stood in the path of three House office buildings, three Senate office buildings, the Supreme Court, three Library of Congress buildings, and parking lots, and so these buildings were lost. A 1967 study, *Capitol Hill Prospectus*, found the following: "In solving its past expansion problems, however, the Congress has also been responsible for the disappearance of some of Capitol Hill's and Washington's oldest and most historic areas. Whole blocks of late 18th and early 19th century dwellings have been demolished to make way for additional Congressional buildings, garages and park areas."

However, several notable early buildings survive. In addition, the Washington Navy Yard, established in 1799, became a major industrial employer, spurring construction of houses and stores nearby.

Highways greatly changed Capitol Hill. By 1955, planners knew that the city needed additional road capacity to handle increasing automobile traffic through its central area and believed that meeting that need required building the Inner Loop Freeway, 17.6 miles of tunnels and elevated open-cut roads, at an estimated cost of $273 million. A section of the freeway, the Southeast–Southwest Freeway (Interstate 695), was completed in the 1960s, consuming 43.19 acres and displacing scores of homes and businesses. Protests and legal action stopped a section that would have run along the west side of Lincoln Park.

Many older retail buildings, movie theaters, and industrial buildings, such as breweries and gas stations, have been replaced by denser office and residential buildings.

The first movie theaters on Capitol Hill were small, typically seating 100 people. Between 1910 and 1939, nine neighborhood theaters opened. Many were demolished to build new, denser projects; one burned; one was demolished for a school parking lot; and one became a church. Larger theaters, like the 1,400-seat Penn built in 1935 and the 900-plus-seat Atlas, built in 1938, survived although substantially modified.

Soon after the city's founding, congregations began building churches, such as Christ Church at 620 G Street SE (1807), and Ebenezer Methodist Church at 415 Fourth Street SE (1810). In 1820, African Americans founded Israel Bethel Colored Methodist Church on First Street SE. By the Civil War, there were Baptist, Methodist, Episcopal, Presbyterian, Catholic, and other denominations and faiths. As congregations outgrew their buildings or members relocated, some church buildings were sold to other congregations, adaptively reused, or demolished.

Because schools in Washington were segregated until the 1954 decision in *Bolling v. Sharpe*, Capitol Hill schools were assigned to either white or African American students. Square 901 (Seventh/Eighth/C/D Streets SE) was originally dedicated to schools for white students. Wallach School, designed by Adolf Cluss, was opened in 1864 (demolished in 1949), followed by Towers School in 1887 and the original Eastern High School in 1892 (converted to Hine Junior High School in 1923), which was replaced by a new Hine School by 1967 that was demolished in 2015. Square 901 was redeveloped in the 2010s.

In the 1890s, the municipal architect built many eight-room schoolhouses, and in the 1940s, the school board began to consolidate these older, smaller schools into larger buildings, for example combining Tyler and Cranch Schools and demolishing the old buildings. Where space permitted, wings were added to the older building, as was done with Maury, Payne, and Bryan Schools. Beginning in the 1930s, the school board acquired lots in the same square as schools and razed buildings to create playing fields or parking lots, such as Hine, Tyler, Logan, Miner, and Payne. Later, some school buildings were declared surplus and sold; some were repurposed as condominiums, like Bryan, Buchanan, and Lovejoy; and others were demolished for redevelopment, for example Hine.

Investors built alley dwellings on Capitol Hill as low-cost rentals for African Americans and immigrants. At its peak in the 1890s, Capitol Hill had as many as 55 inhabited alleys. Reform movements beginning in the 19th century targeted alley dwellings as unsafe, unsanitary, and a public safety risk, and many were demolished. Some were replaced by public housing, such as Navy Place SE. In 1892, Congress restricted new alley dwellings to wider alleys and required sewerage, water mains, and light. No new alley dwellings were built on Capitol Hill after 1893. First Ladies Ellen Wilson and Eleanor Roosevelt advocated eliminating alley dwellings. The Alley Dwelling Authority was created in 1934 with a mandate to discontinue alley dwellings by 1944 and to care for displaced alley residents. Responding to a wartime housing shortage, the deadline was extended to 1955, and after homeowners living in alleys successfully lobbied, the prohibition was repealed in 1954. There are approximately 30 new and historic inhabited alleys on Capitol Hill.

H Street NE, once the second-most-valuable commercial district in the city, was devastated by the riots following the assassination of Dr. Martin Luther King Jr. in 1968. Of 374 businesses on H Street, 122 were damaged, including 53 that were 50-to-100-percent destroyed. Citywide, 13 people died, 5,000 lost work, and 2,000 lost homes. Leading up to the riots, many African Americans suffered poor living conditions, and one in four families lived below the poverty line, crowded into substandard housing. Many were unemployed or underemployed, especially in areas later hit hardest by the riots. Public transportation to suburban employment centers was inadequate. Only one in three public high school students graduated. The public hospital was crowded. These conditions led to tensions, disturbances at public events, and confrontations involving the police. After the riots, the government of the District of Columbia declared H Street an urban renewal area and began revitalization efforts. In the 2000s, H Street began to return to prosperity.

Although riots and redevelopment took a toll on Capitol Hill's built environment, a large number of 19th- and early-20th-century buildings survive.

CHAPTER 1

Early Buildings

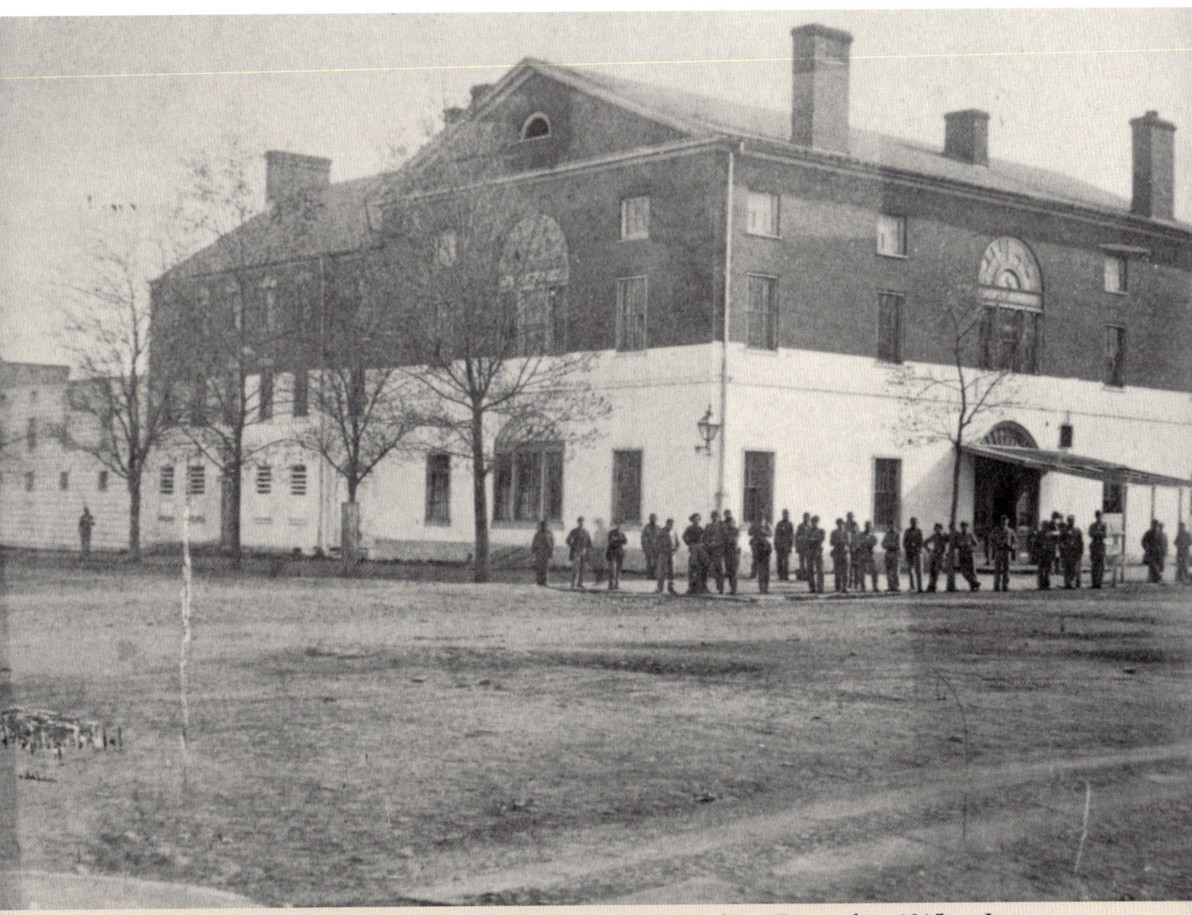

After the British army burned the Capitol in 1814, Washington residents, fearing Congress would move the capital back to Philadelphia, built a replacement "Brick Capitol" at the corner of First and A Streets NE. Congress met here from December 1815 to January 1817. (Photograph by Matthew Brady; courtesy Historical Society of Washington, DC, CHS-03740.)

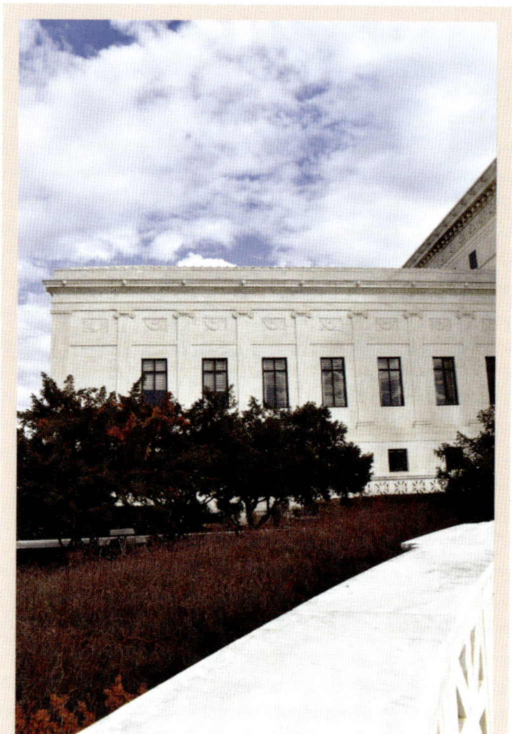

The Brick Capitol, at First and A Streets NE, after use as a prison during the Civil War, was converted into row houses in 1869 and referred to as Trumbull's Row. Later, the building served as the headquarters of the National Woman's Party before being demolished in 1935 for the Supreme Court building. (Courtesy Historical Society of Washington, DC, CHS-03742.)

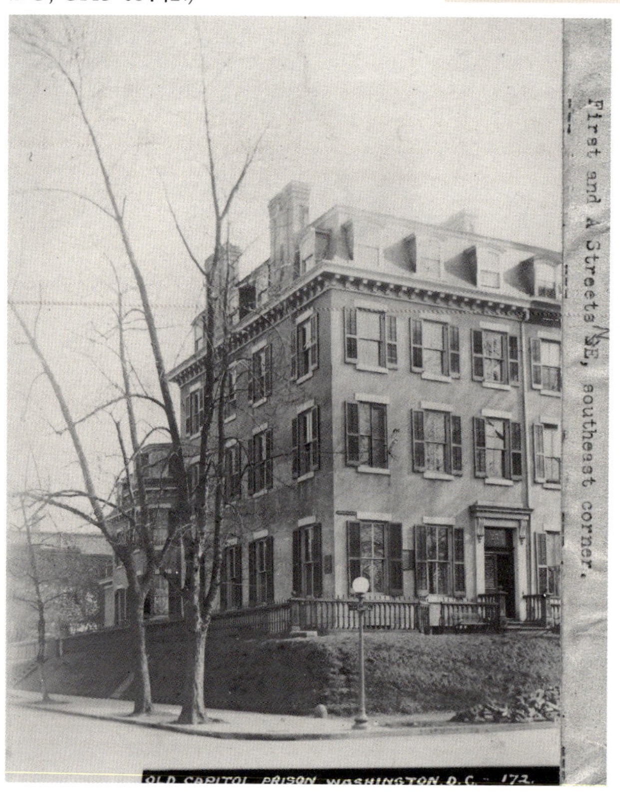

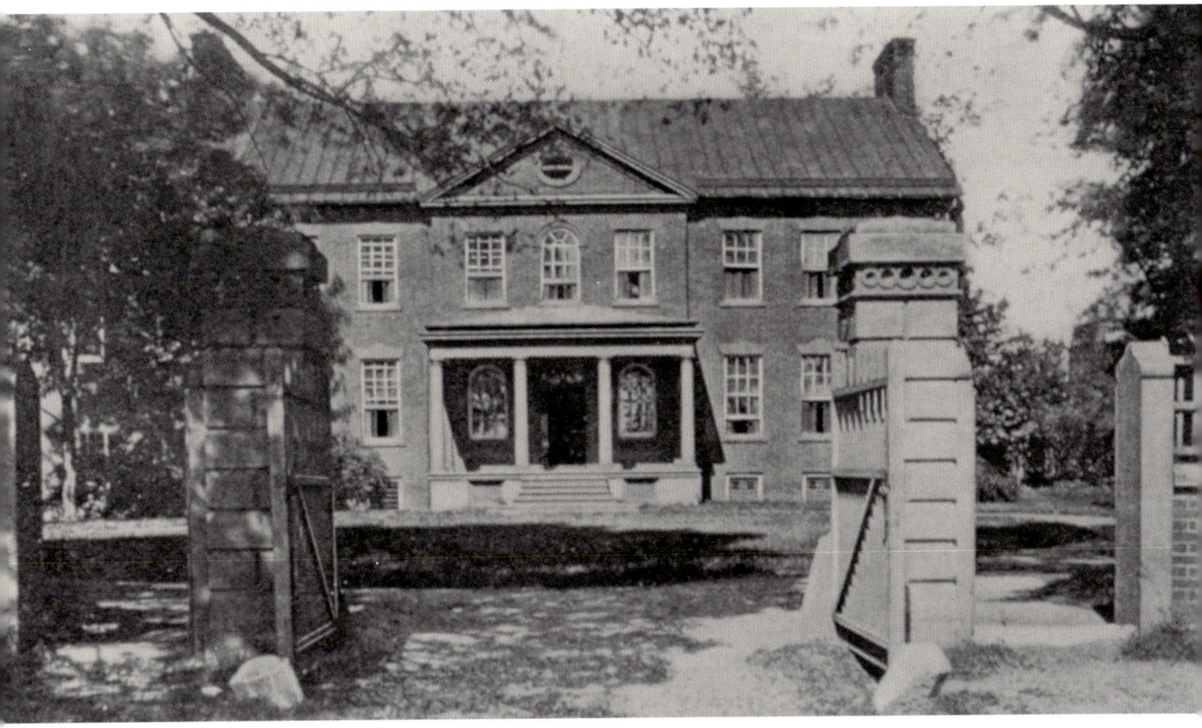

Daniel Carroll of Duddington, one of the city's original landowners and known for his dispute with Pierre L'Enfant over building a house in a street, rebuilt his mansion in Square 736, seen around 1880. The Carroll family owned the land until 1886. The mansion was demolished, and in 1890, Archimedes Heckman bought the entire square and laid out 146 row house lots and a new street, Heckman Street (now Duddington Place). Duddington Mansion was behind these row houses at 138–142 F Street SE. (Courtesy LOC, LOT 11800-A-1, G-890.)

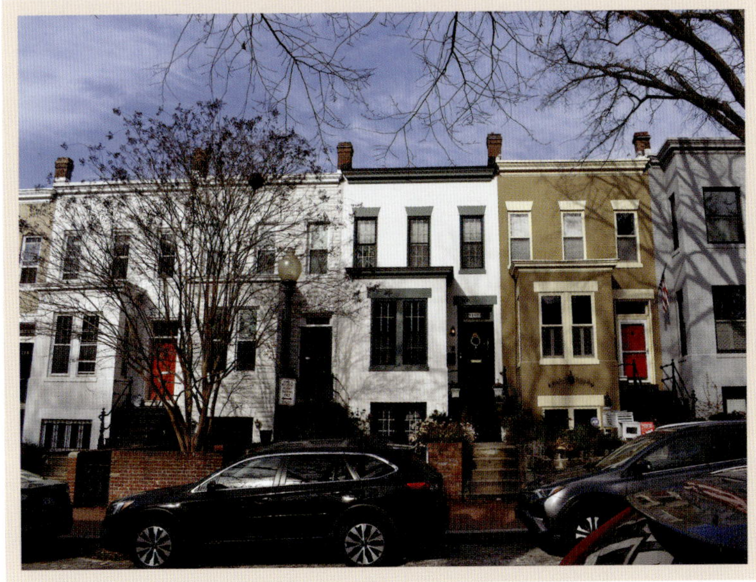

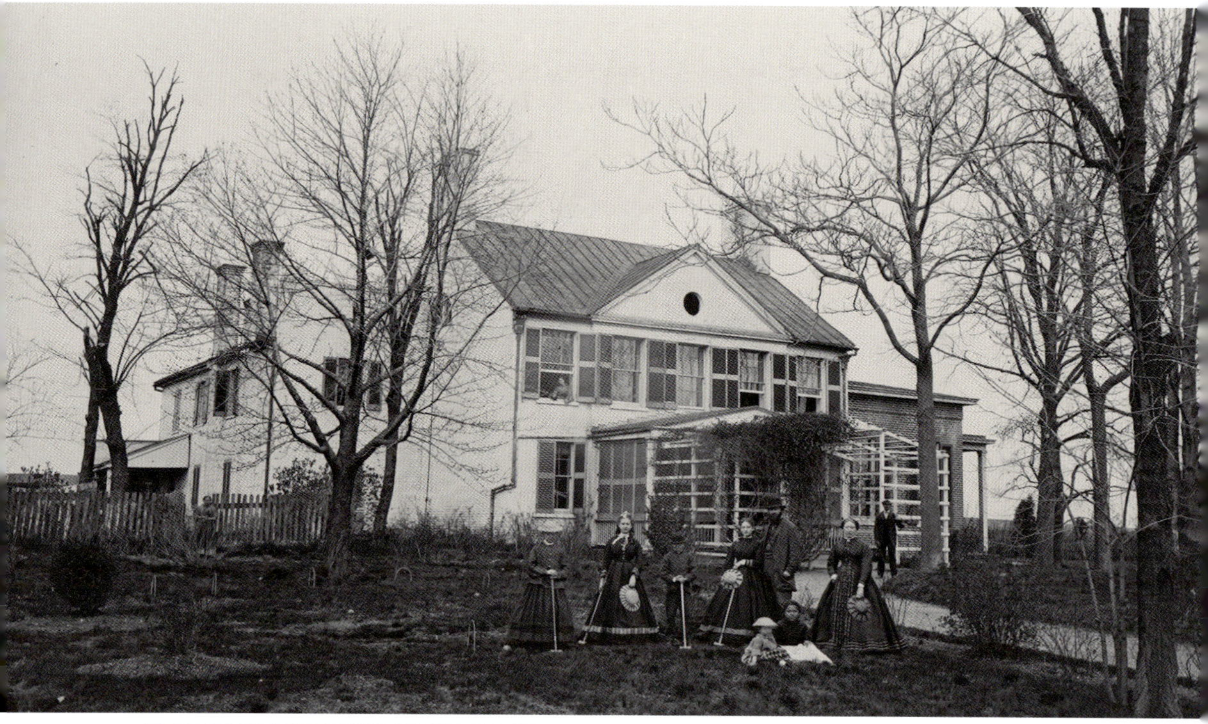

In 1796, William Mayne Duncanson built a brick house, the Maples, at 630 South Carolina Avenue SE, seen in 1862. Later owners included Francis Scott Key, Maj. Augustus A. Nicholson, and Sen. John M. Clayton. In 1871, Emily Edson Briggs (1830–1910), known for her "Olivia" columns during the Civil War, bought Maple Square and lived there for 40 years. A settlement house operated here between 1927 and 2010. It is now part of a residential development. (Courtesy LOC, LC-B817-7745.)

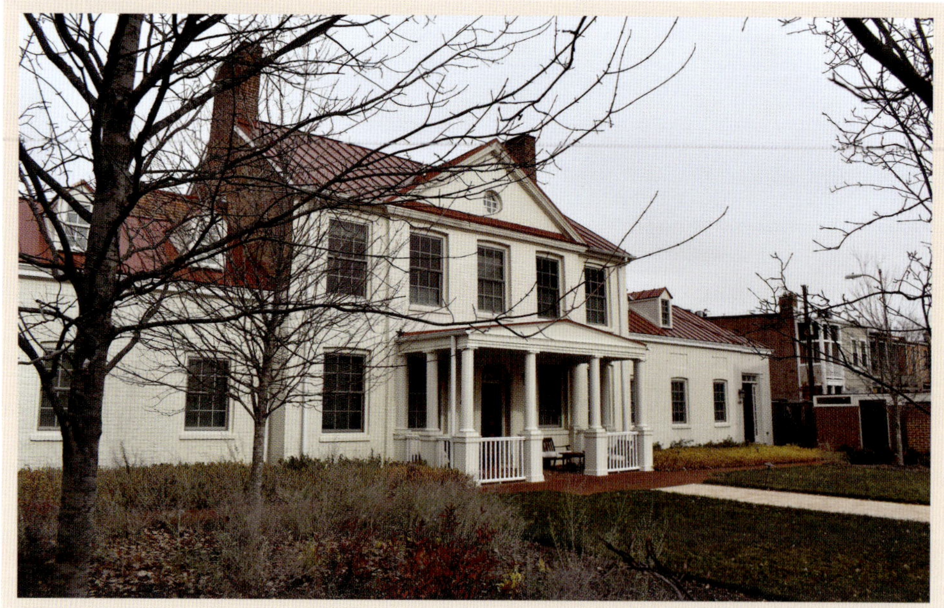

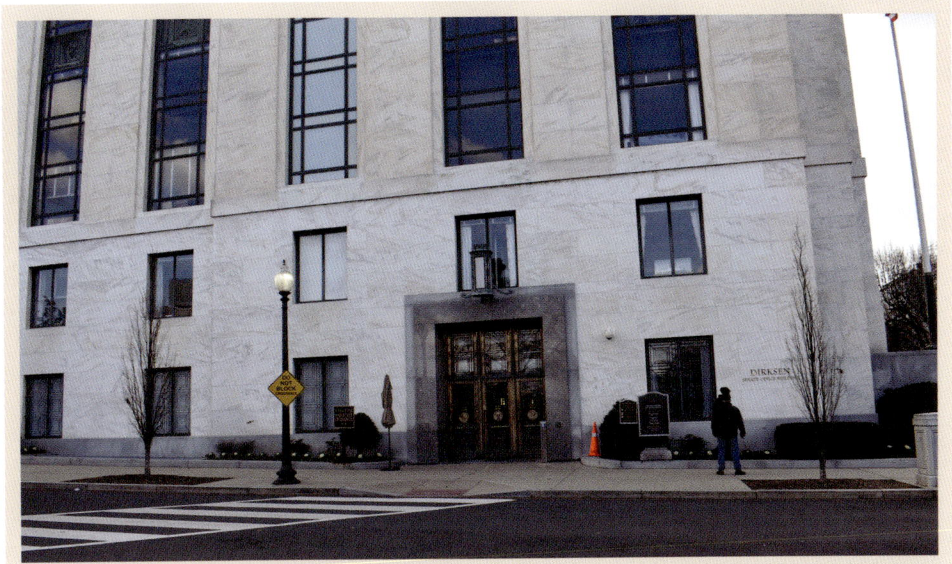

James Greenleaf (1765–1843) contracted to buy lots, defaulted on his payments, and litigated to retain them in 13 Supreme Court cases. In 1831 or earlier, Greenleaf built a frame house at First and C Streets NE in Square 725, photographed around 1870. The house was well-furnished, with a large library, and he had a stable, horses, and cows. The Dirksen Senate Office Building (1958) occupies the site today. (Courtesy Historical Society of Washington, DC, CHS-03744.)

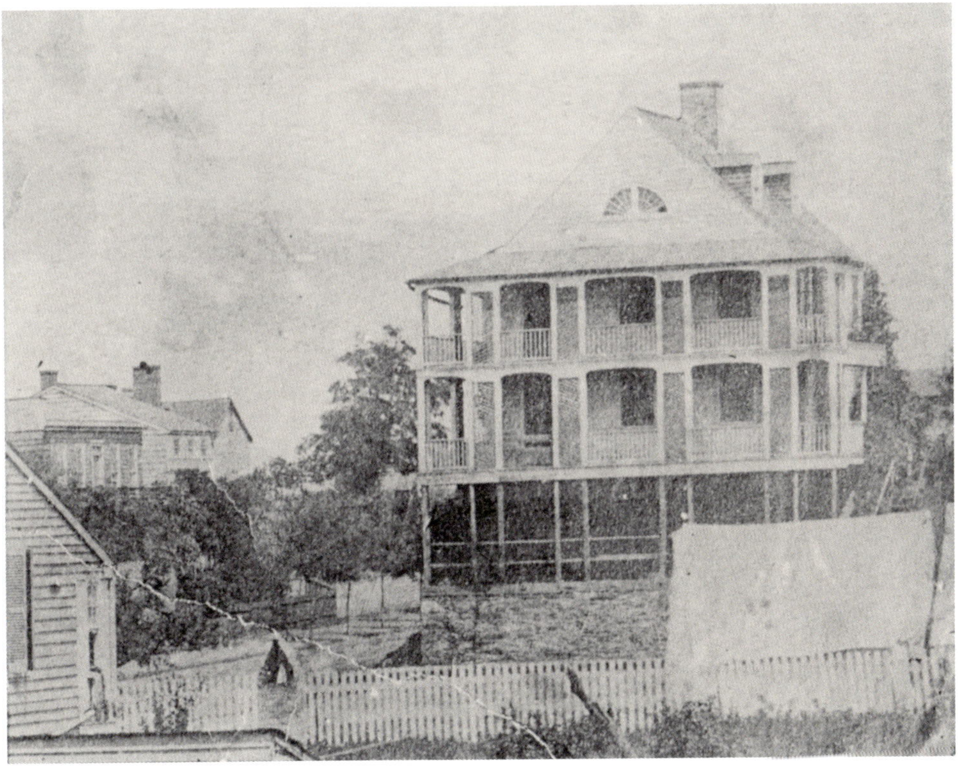

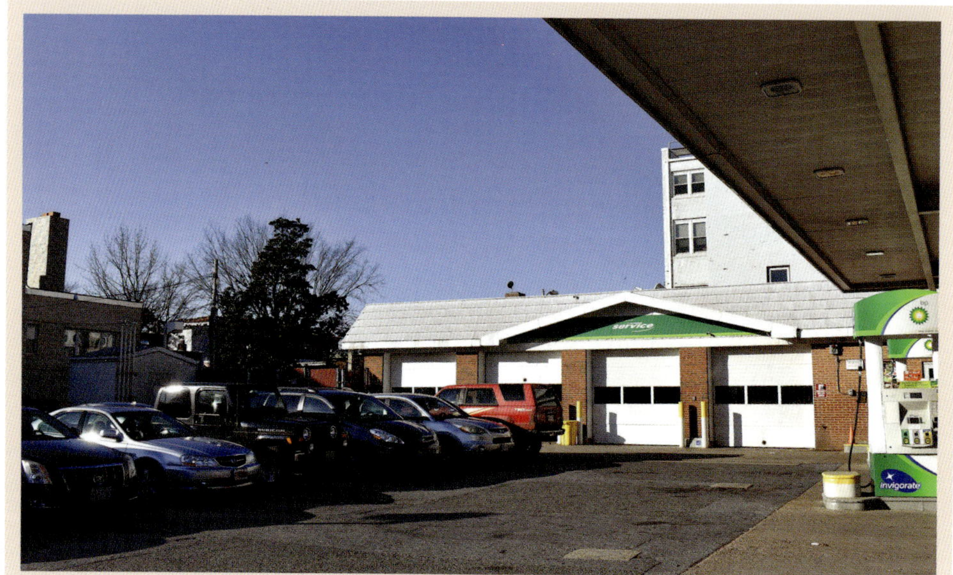

Tunnicliff's Hotel, at Ninth Street and Pennsylvania Avenue SE in Square 925, opened in 1795. William Tunnicliff ran it until 1798. The building later functioned as a hotel, private home, and, as shown on an 1888 map, a beer garden. This photograph was taken between 1909 and 1936. It was demolished in 1936. Distad's BP, at 823 Pennsylvania Avenue SE, now occupies the site. (Courtesy LOC, LC-F-8112-44647.)

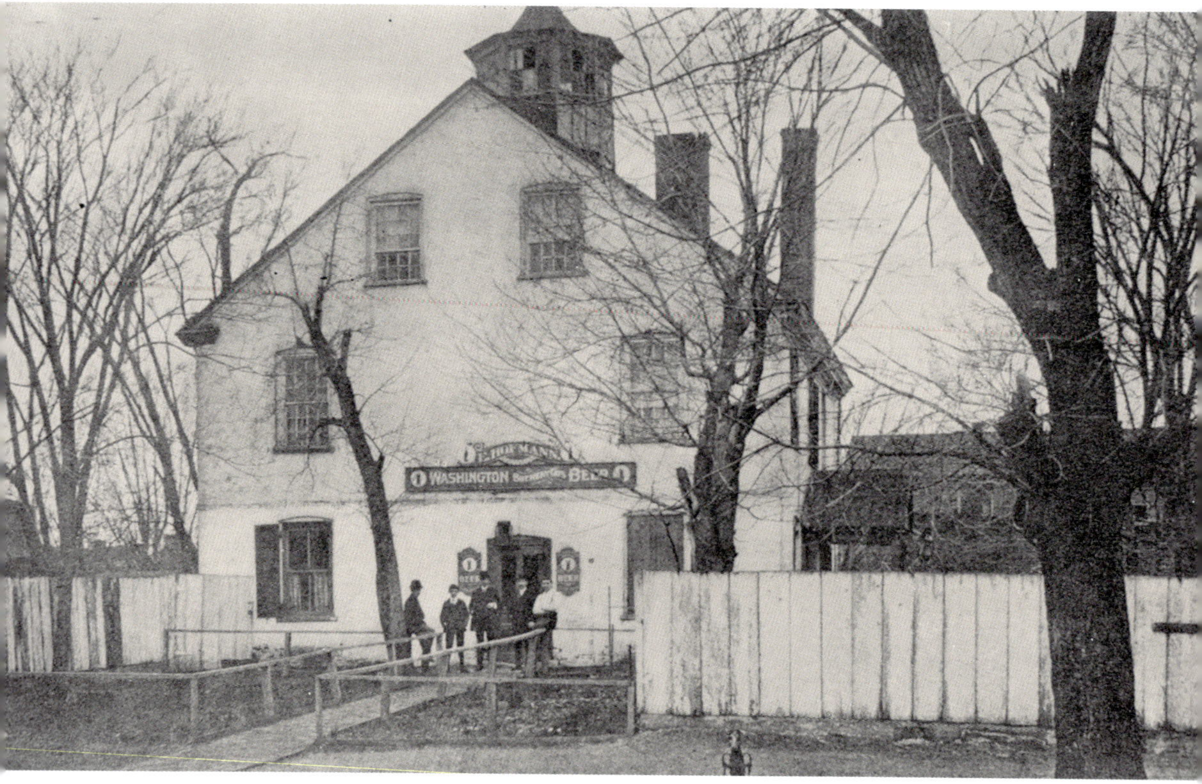

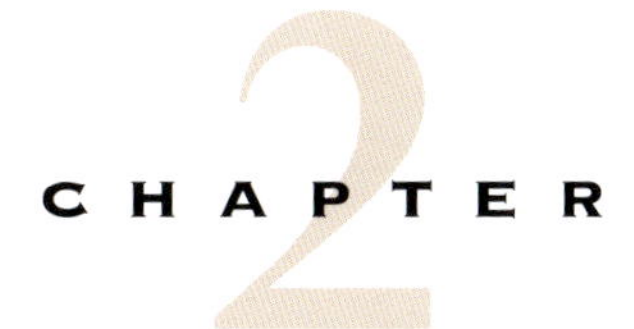

Chapter 2

Libraries, Offices, Parking, and Parks

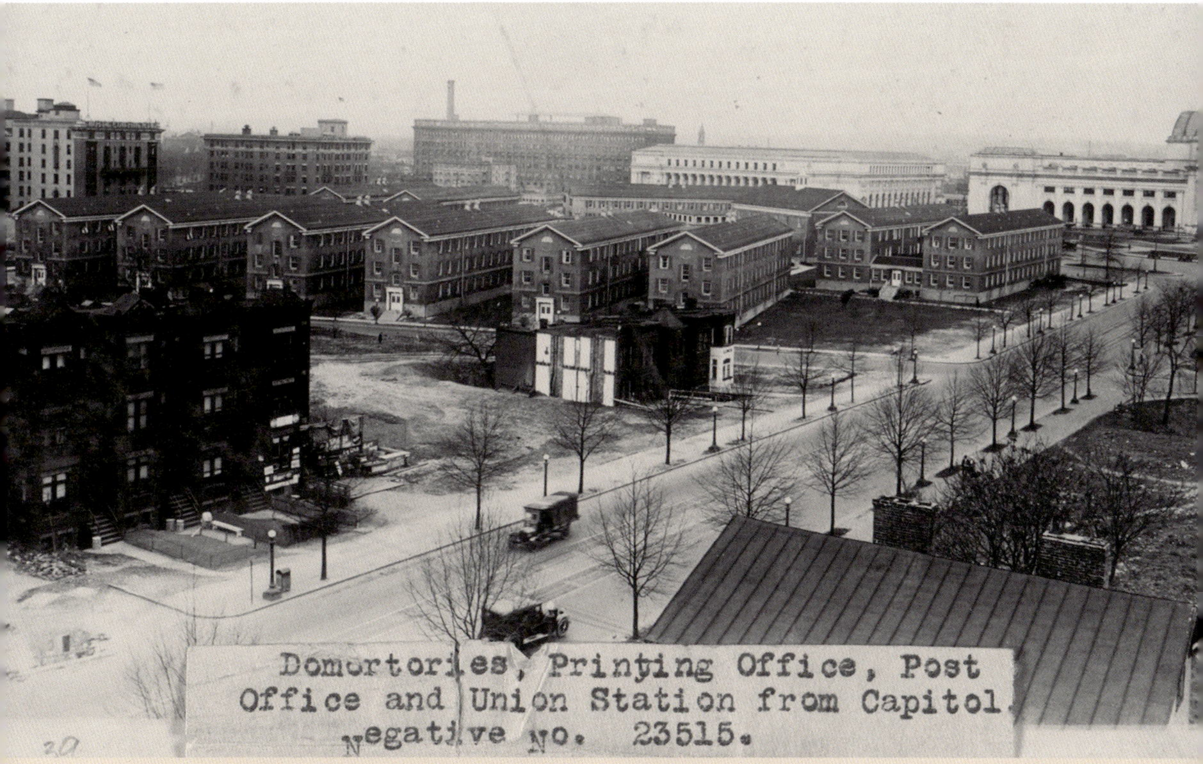

Domortories, Printing Office, Post Office and Union Station from Capitol. Negative No. 23515.

The Union Plaza Dormitories south of Union Station were built during World War I to house women working for the federal government. In the distance are, from left to right, the government printing office, post office, and Union Station. The dormitories were demolished in 1930 for the North Capitol Park. (Courtesy LOC, LOT 123517-6.)

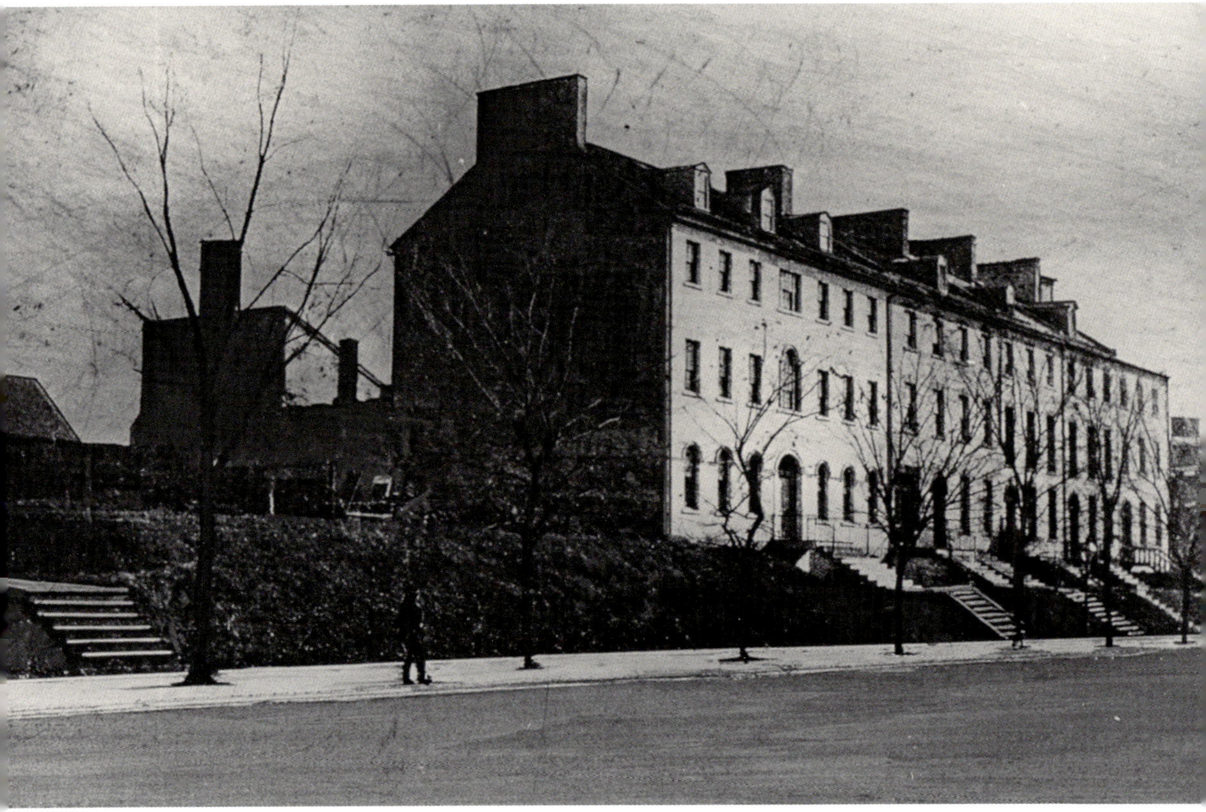

In 1798, Daniel Carroll of Duddington built Carroll Row, five three-story brick row houses at First and A Streets SE, and marketed them as elite rentals for members of Congress. The project was a success, attracting a series of distinguished hotel managers. Congressman Abraham Lincoln boarded here in 1848. Carroll Row, photographed around 1875, was razed in 1887 to build the Jefferson Building of the Library of Congress. (Courtesy Historical Society of Washington, DC, GLS-A02.)

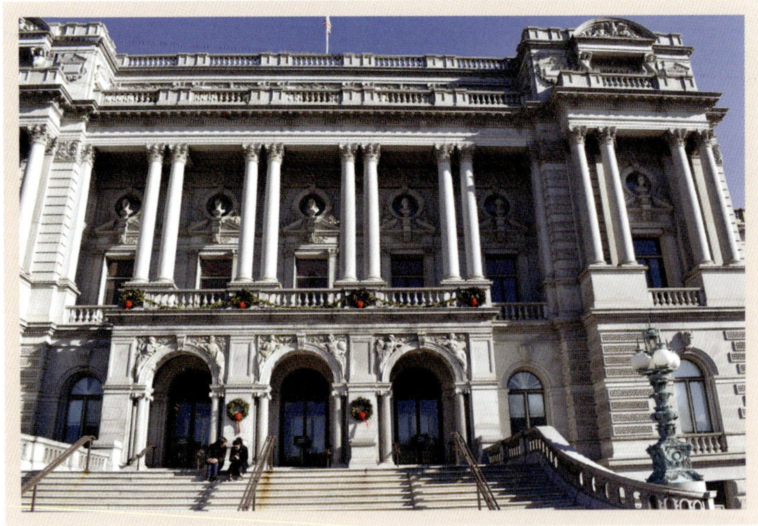

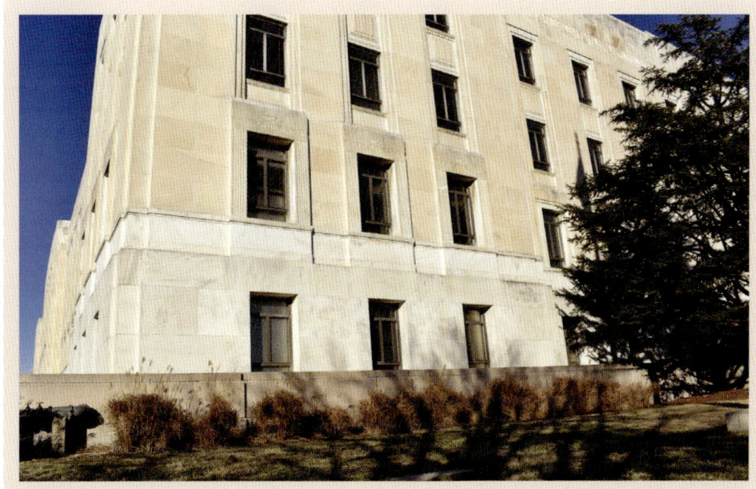

Elias B. Caldwell (1776–1825), the clerk of the Supreme Court, built this house at 206 Pennsylvania Avenue SE in 1809. Seen between 1910 and 1919, it had a wedge-shaped addition. The Church of the Reformation is partly visible on the right. The house and all buildings in Square 761 were demolished by 1938 to construct the Adams Building of the Library of Congress. (Photograph by Joseph E. Bishop; courtesy Historical Society of Washington, DC, BI-040.)

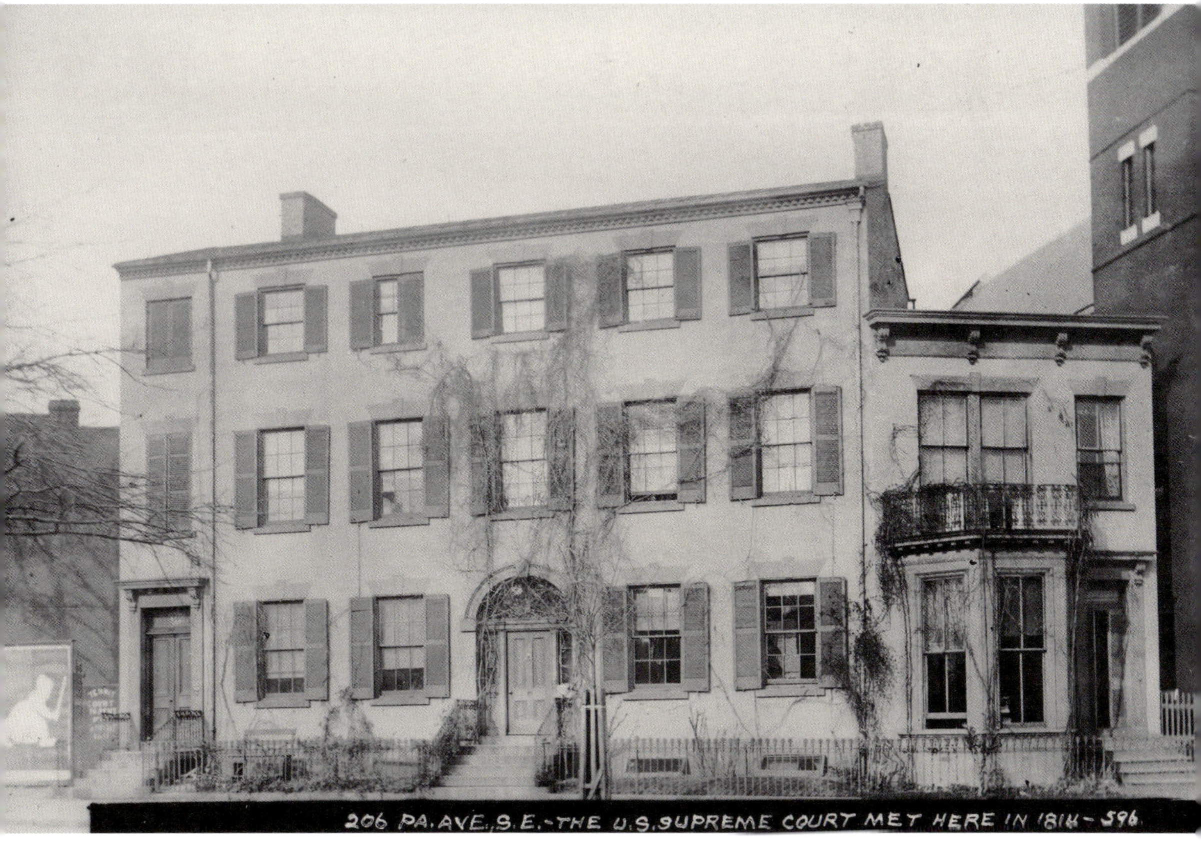

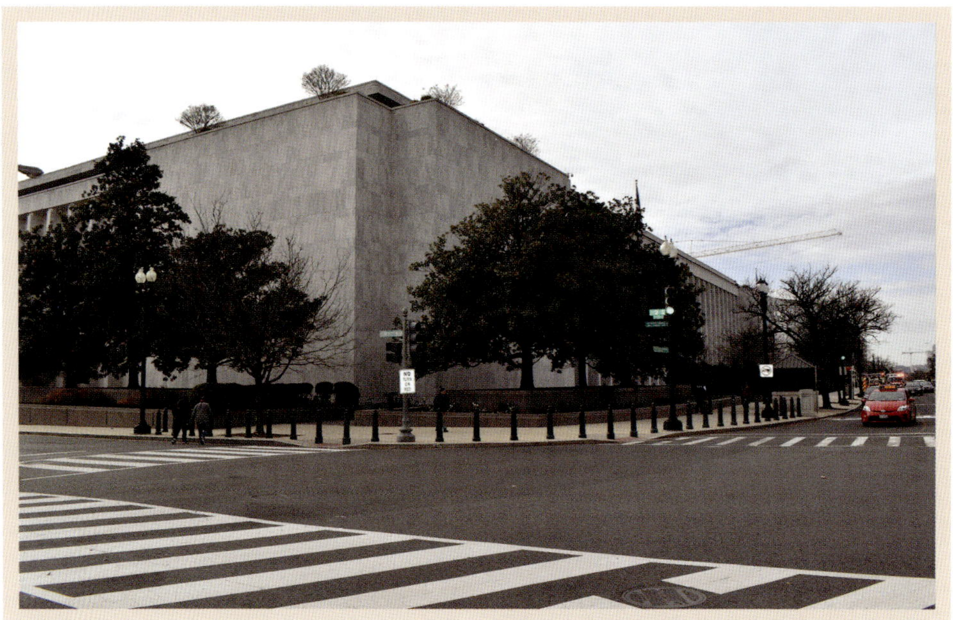

This 1949 photograph shows the corner building, DiCiero's Restaurant, at 151–153 Independence Avenue SE, and to the right, Rector's Restaurant, Angelo's Restaurant, and the Neptune Grill. Nearby stores offered gifts, drugs, clothing, flowers, fruit, and liquor. All of these buildings, together with 100 more in Square 732, were demolished in the 1960s to build the Madison Building of the Library of Congress. (Photograph by John P. Wymer; courtesy Historical Society of Washington, DC, WY-1644.)

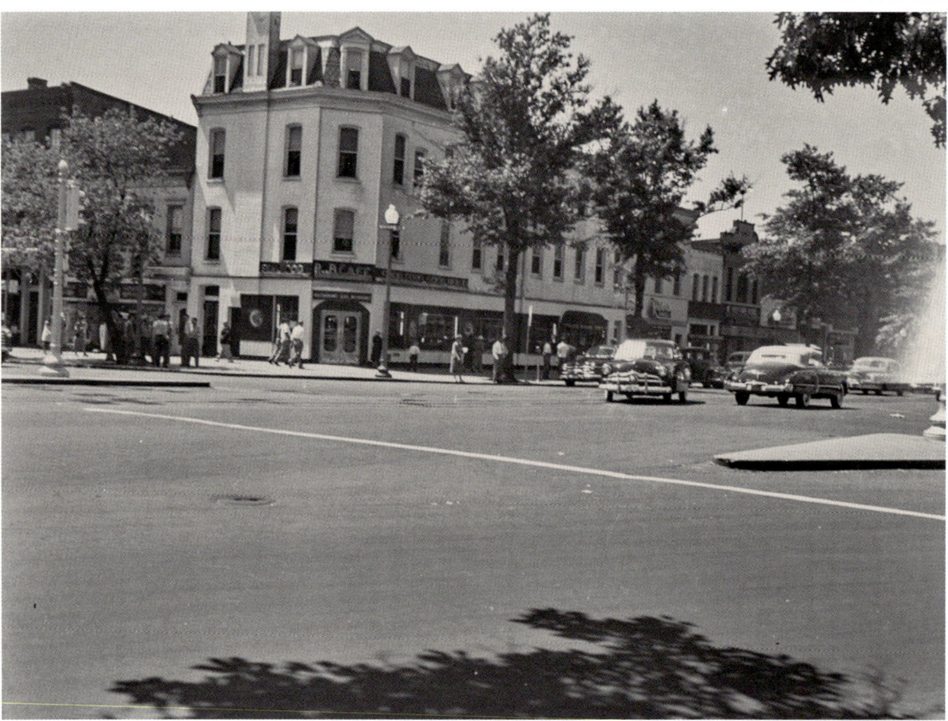

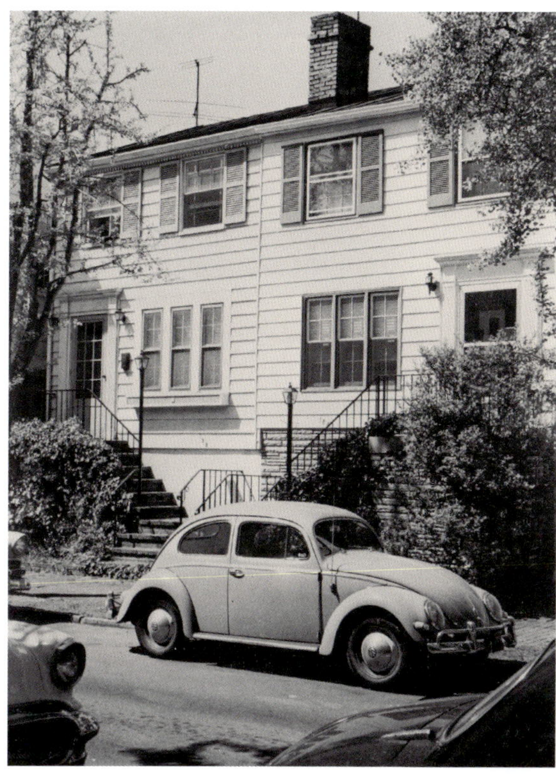

Carroll Street SE was one of Capitol Hill's one-block streets running east to west in Square 732. These frame row houses at 122–124 Carroll Street SE, seen in 1959, were two of 40 houses on the street and were built before 1880. The nonhistorical first-story windows were typical postwar renovations. The square was razed for the Madison Building of the Library of Congress in the 1960s. (Photograph by W. Bailey; courtesy LOC, HABS DC,WASH-147.)

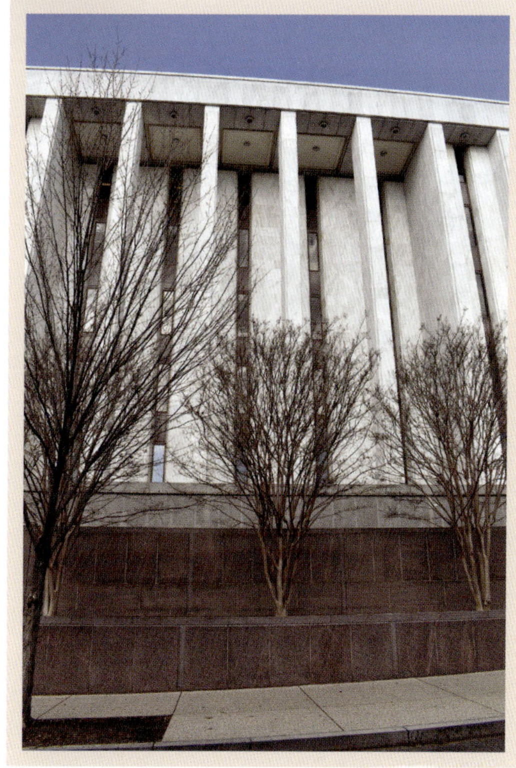

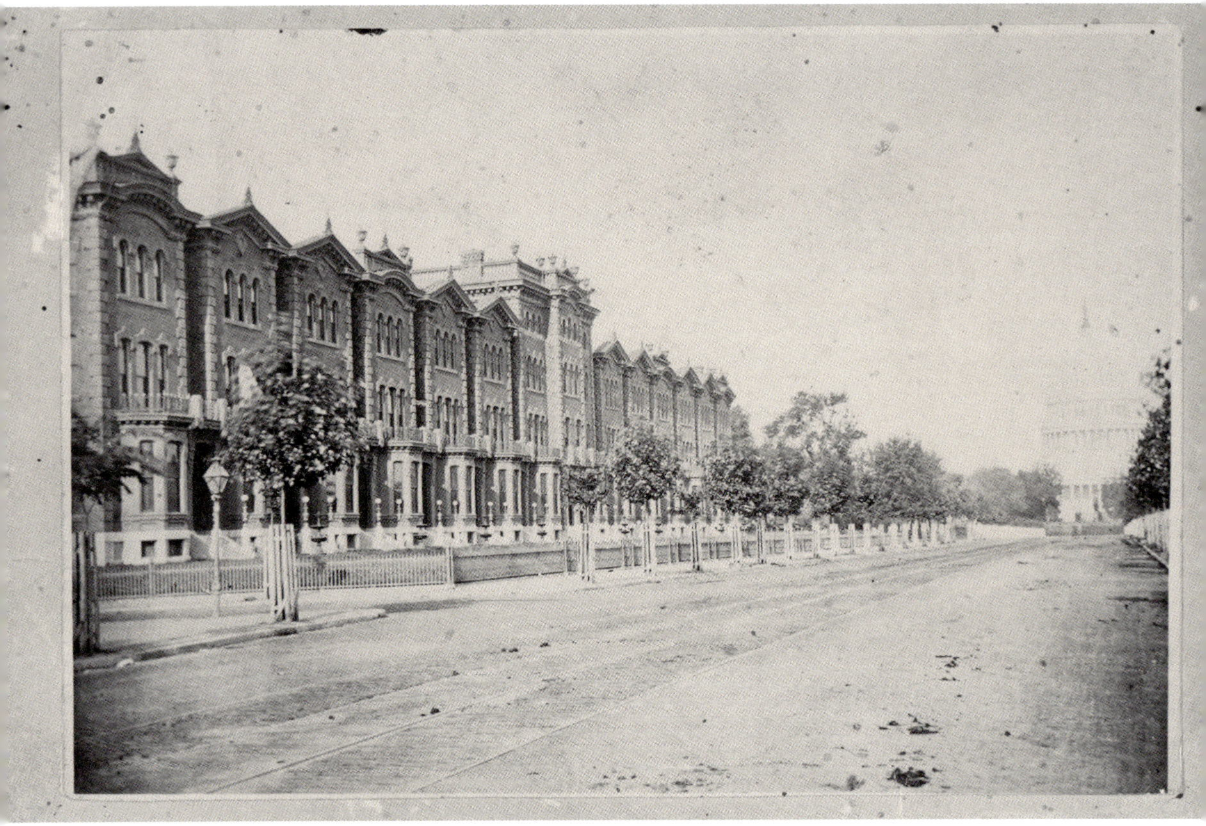

George H. Griebel designed these 14 opulent row houses on the 200 block of East Capitol Street SE in 1871 for Capt. Albert Grant, photographed around 1874. These Grant's Row houses were demolished in 1929 and replaced by the Folger Shakespeare Library, housing the Folger Shakespeareana collection. Paul Phillipe Cret designed the Stripped Classical building, widely considered exceptional in design both inside and out. (Photograph by M.P. Rice; courtesy LOC, PR 13 CN 1989:121.)

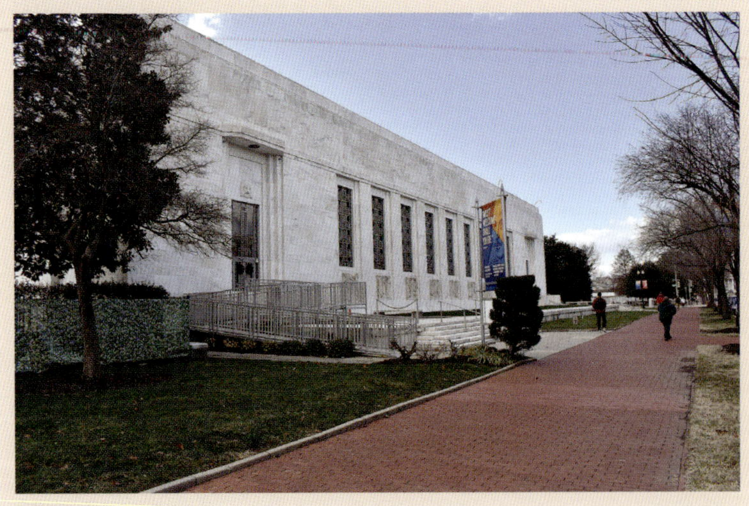

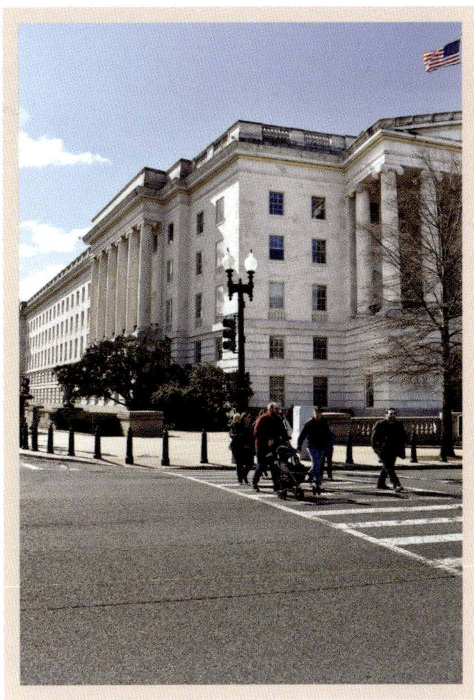

In 1874, Gen. Benjamin F. Butler, a controversial Civil War figure, built a four-story stone house, the Gray House, at 3 B Street (Independence Avenue) SE. Sen. John P. Jones rented part of the house and hosted Pres. Chester A. Arthur, who lived here between September and December 1881 while the White House was redecorated. In 1933, the Longworth House Office Building replaced the house. (Photograph by Willard R. Ross; courtesy Historical Society of Washington, DC, CHS-04544.)

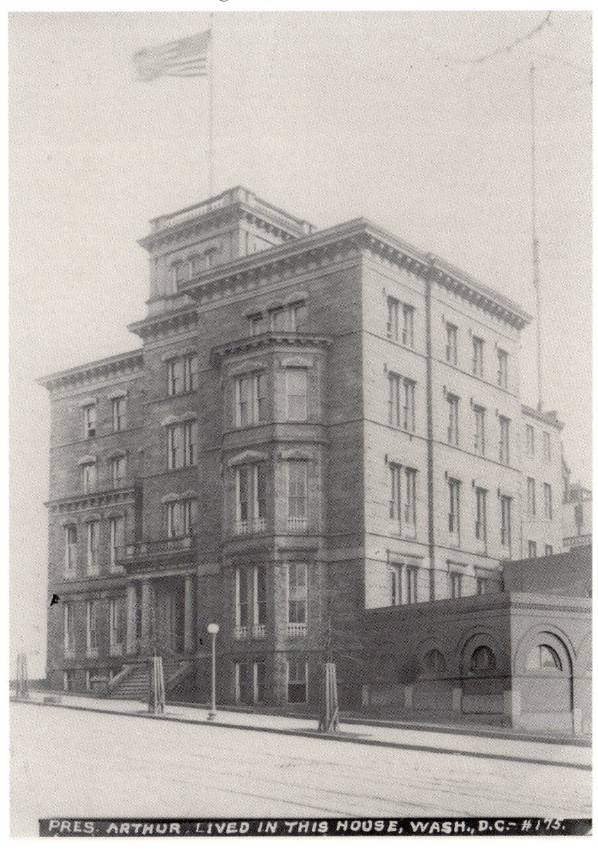

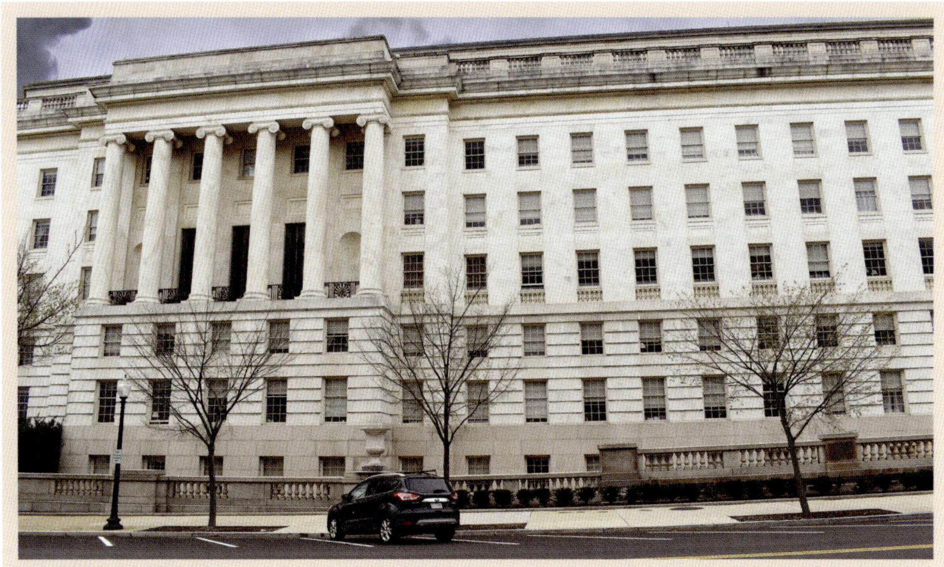

The US Coast and Geodetic Survey is a federal agency originally established in 1807 to survey the East Coast. Now, it defines and manages a national coordinate system that serves as a basis for many applications of science and engineering. Its building at 205 New Jersey Avenue SE, seen between around 1905 and 1930, was demolished for the Longworth House Office Building. (Courtesy LOC, LC-H25-3522.)

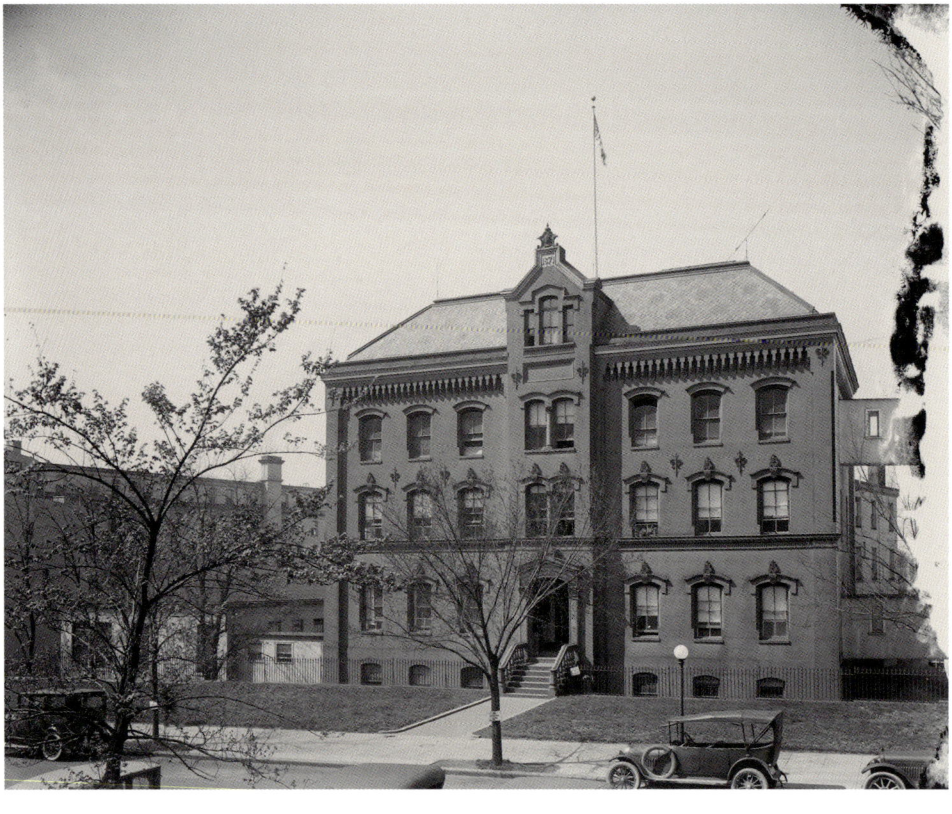

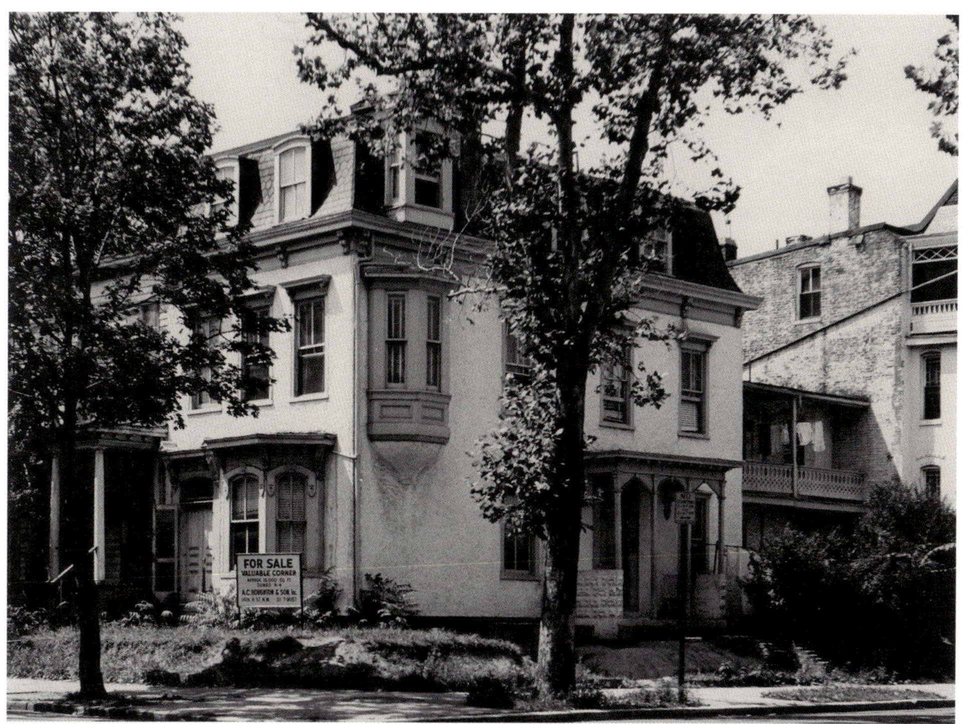

Harry B. Mathiot (1856–1926), a gardener, lived at 230 A Street NE beginning around 1910. His widow remained here until 1940. The Marlow Coal Company, which had operated a coal yard on the block since the 1870s, bought the house in 1955 and demolished it for a Supreme Court parking lot. In 1982, the federal government bought it to preserve the parking lot. (Photograph by William E. Barret; courtesy Historical Society of Washington, DC, KC-4306.)

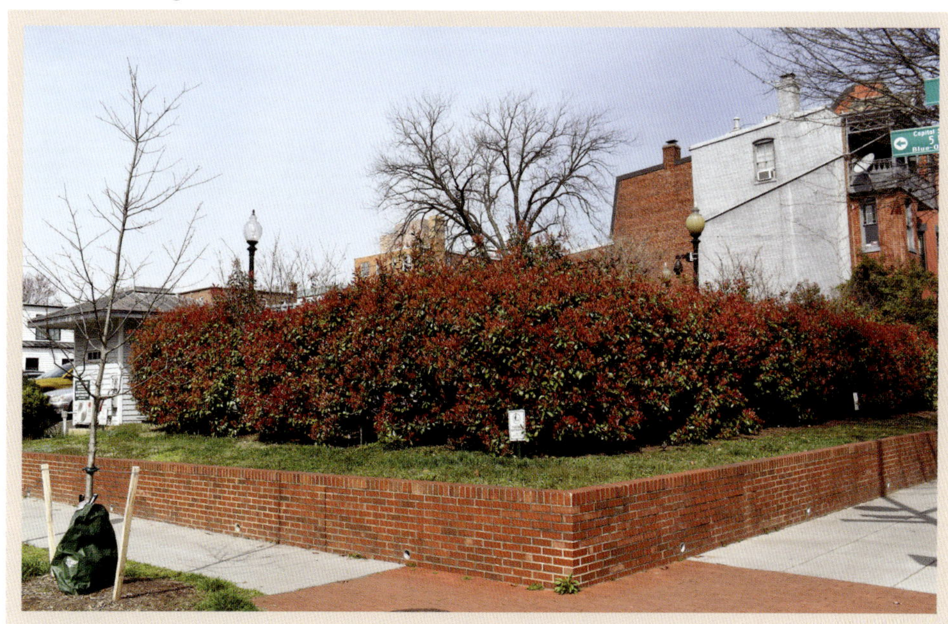

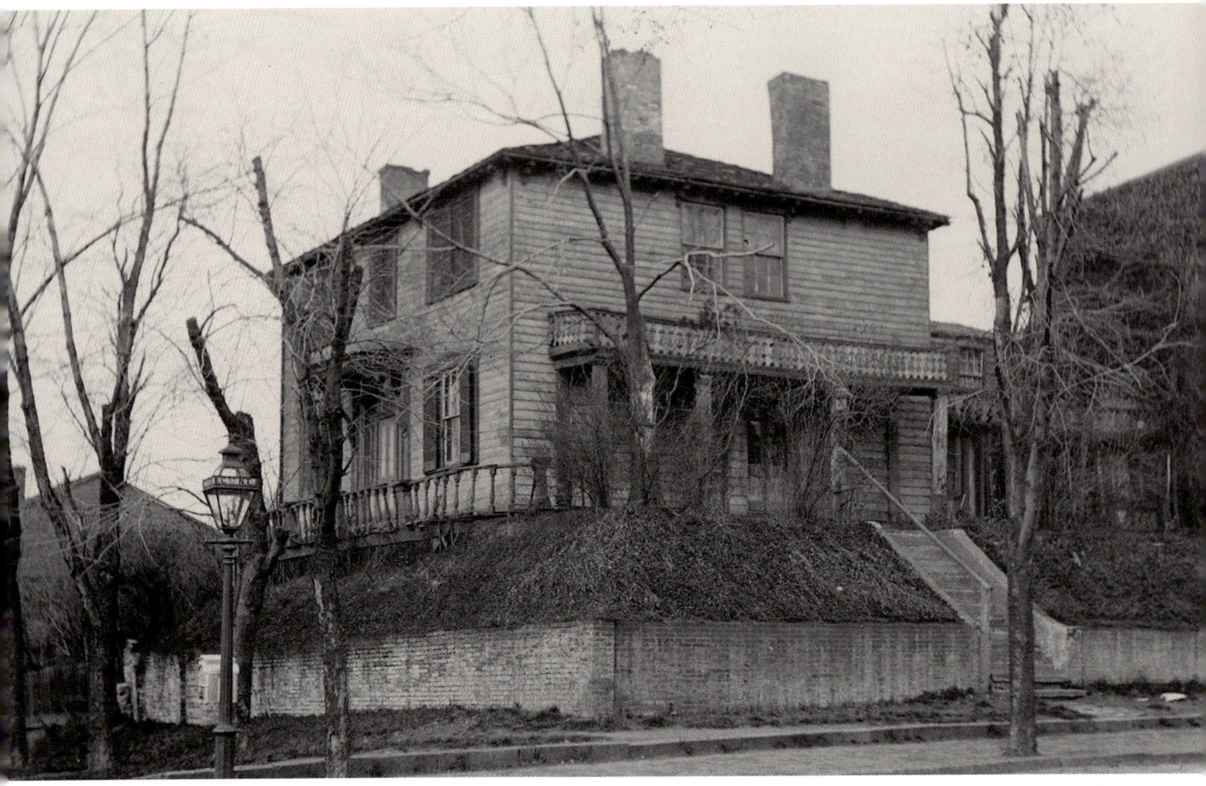

This frame house at 100 C Street NE, photographed between 1918 and 1920, was built in 1858 or earlier. Julia Martin, a clerk at the Department of the Treasury and active supporter of the temperance movement, lived here from 1870 until her death in 1903 at age 78. William E. Gatton, a saloonkeeper, lived here in 1906. The site is now in Senate Lot No. 19. The Capitol Police Headquarters is in the background. (Courtesy LOC, LC-F-2541.)

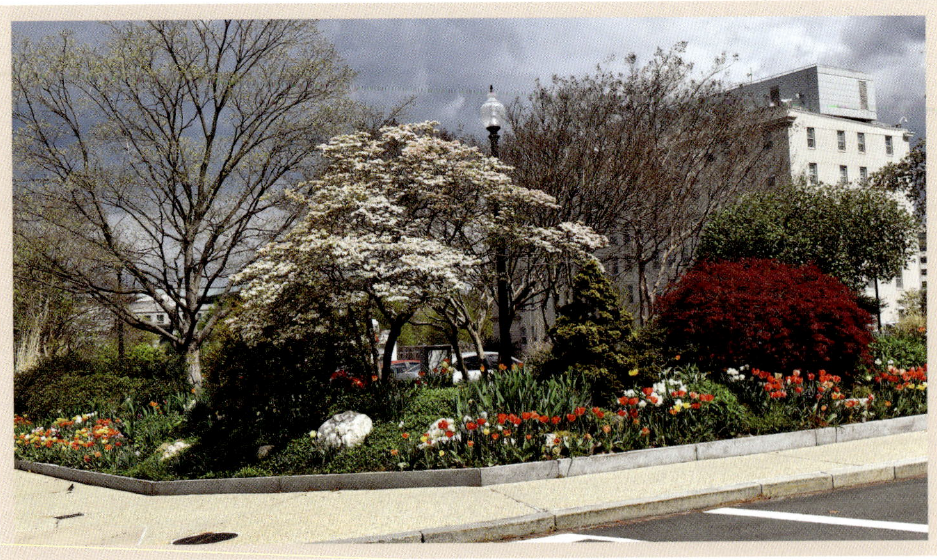

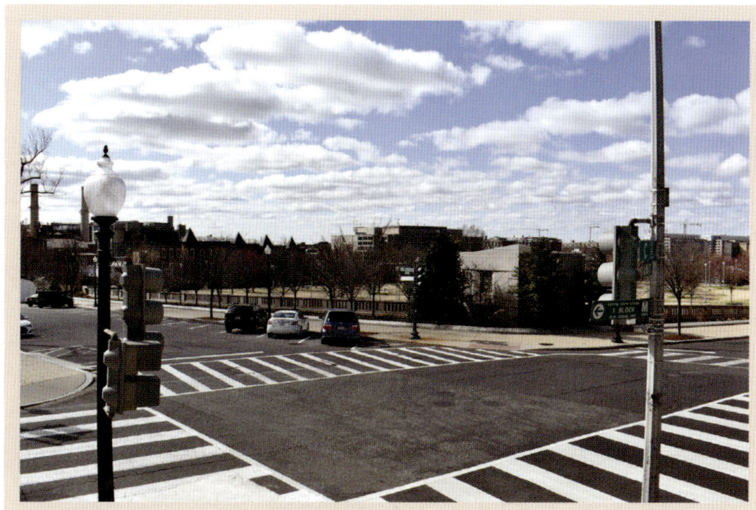

The George Washington Inn at New Jersey Avenue and C Street SE, pictured between 1910 and 1925, was a fashionable apartment hotel offering one- and two-bedroom and bath apartments (without housekeeping) by the day, week, or month. Its dining room was popular, and the hotel hosted society wedding receptions. It closed in 1956 and was demolished in 1964 for the Spirit of Justice Park/parking garage. (Courtesy LOC, LD-F82.)

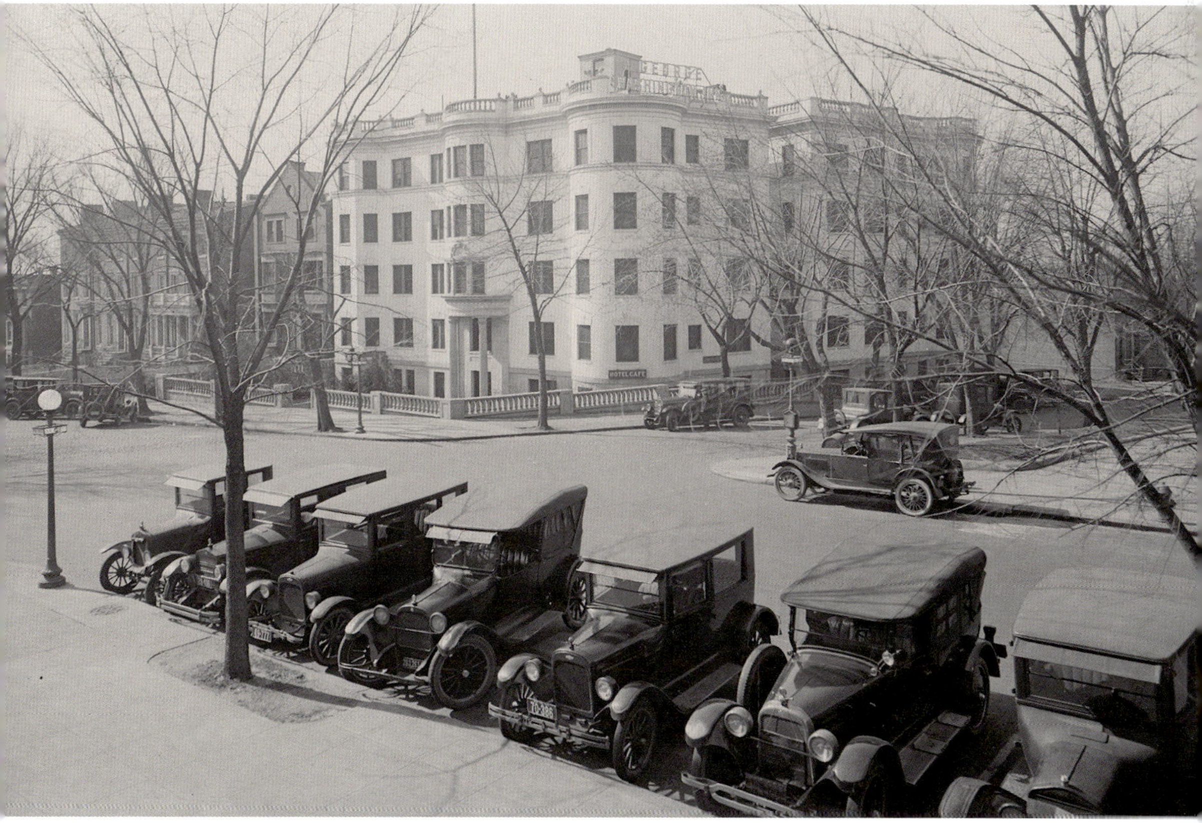

The brick house at 309 New Jersey Avenue SE was built in 1888 or earlier. From about 1934 to 1948, Effie P. McCombe (1884–1948) operated the Capitol View Tourist Home here, offering furnished rooms, "a home away from home." In 1968, the Spirit of Justice Park, a green-roofed parking garage for Congress, was built covering all of Square 691. The House East Fountain appears in the center of the photograph. (Author's collection.)

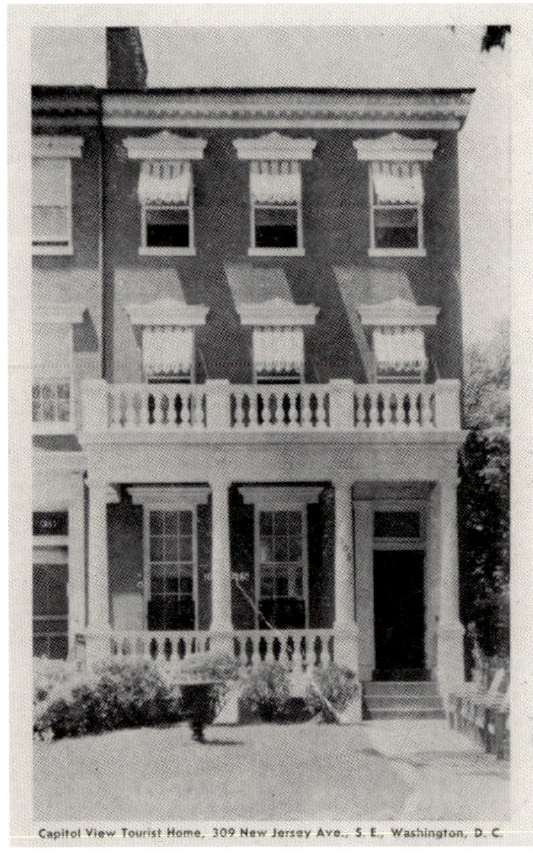

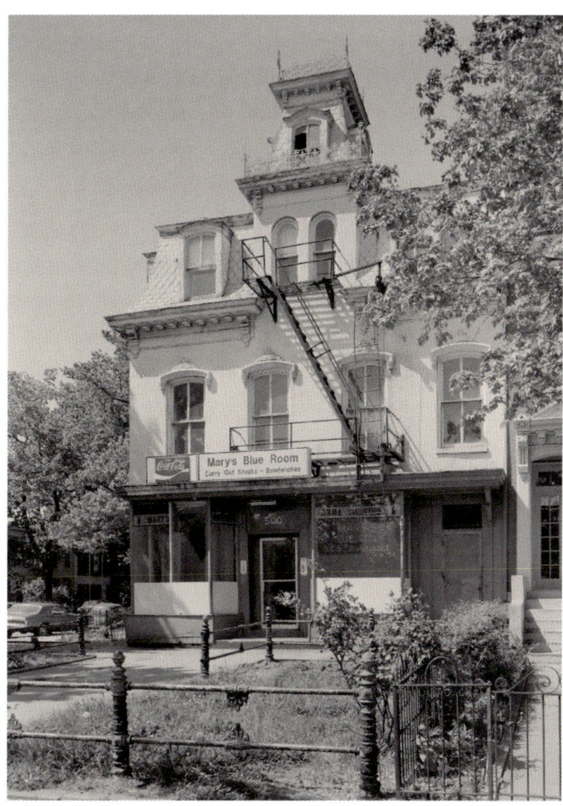

The house at 500 East Capitol Street, built in 1879, exemplified Second Empire architecture and was the home of Wellans' Restaurant and later Mary's Blue Room, a diner. Over strong community opposition, it was demolished in 1972 for a church parking lot. This loss spurred establishing the Capitol Hill Historic District in 1976. In 1995, Eric Colbert designed a new row house for this corner. (Photograph by Jack E. Boucher; courtesy LOC, HABS DC,WASH-379.)

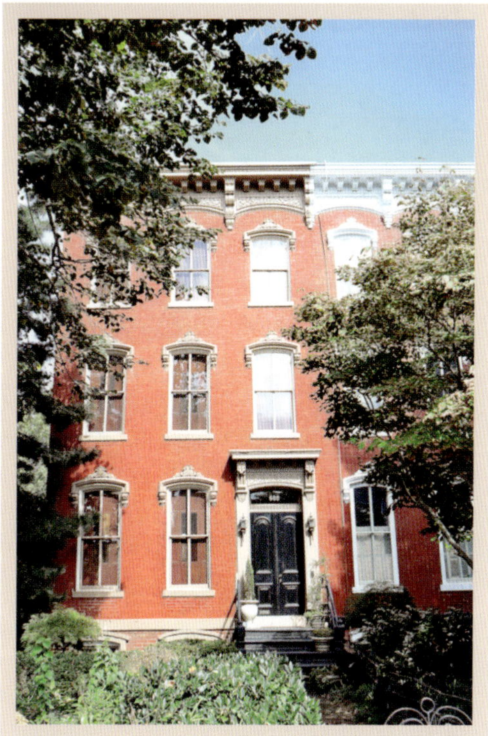

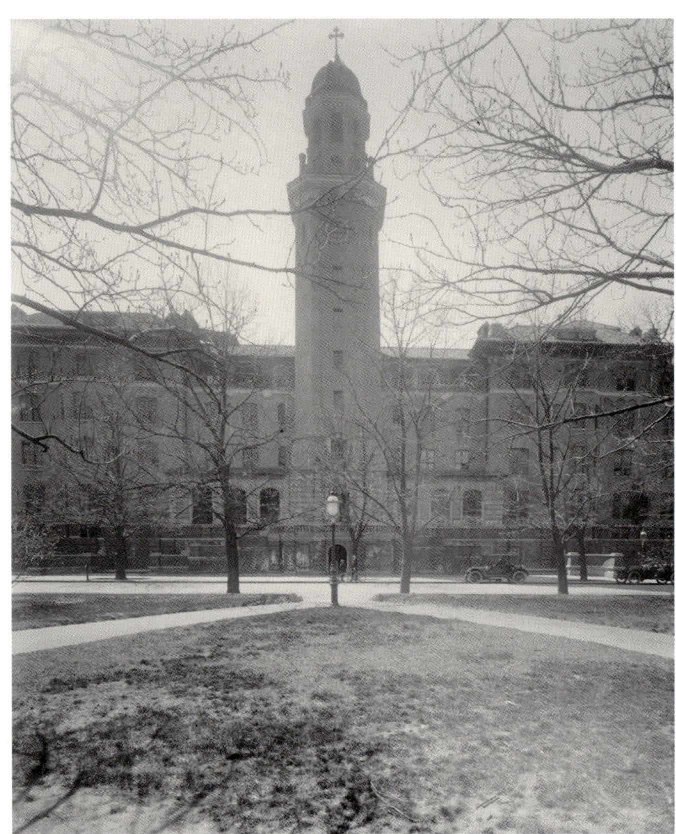

Providence Hospital was founded by a religious order in 1861. Until 1956, the hospital occupied Square 764 (Second/Third/D/E Streets SE). It is shown here between 1910 and 1926. When a new hospital was needed, it was built at 1150 Varnum Street NE in 1956; it closed in 2019. After the hospital was demolished in 1964, proposals for 10-story buildings or a parking lot failed. In 1973, Congress bought the square as a park, pending building a Congressional page school, which was later abandoned. (Courtesy LOC, LC-F82-1053A.)

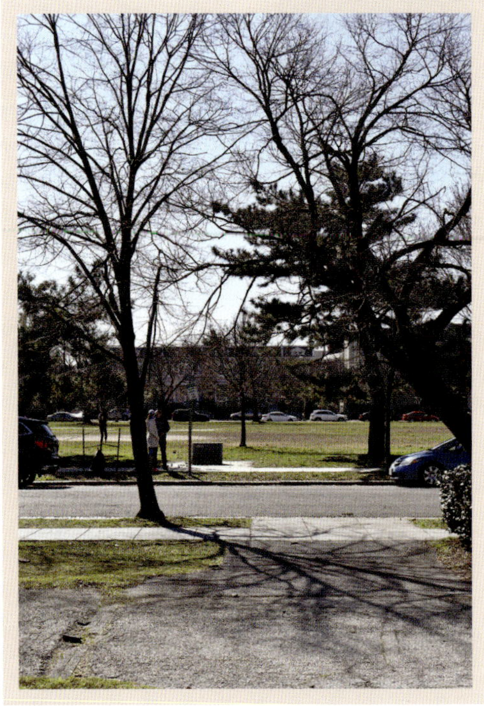

CHAPTER 3

A Freeway Runs through It

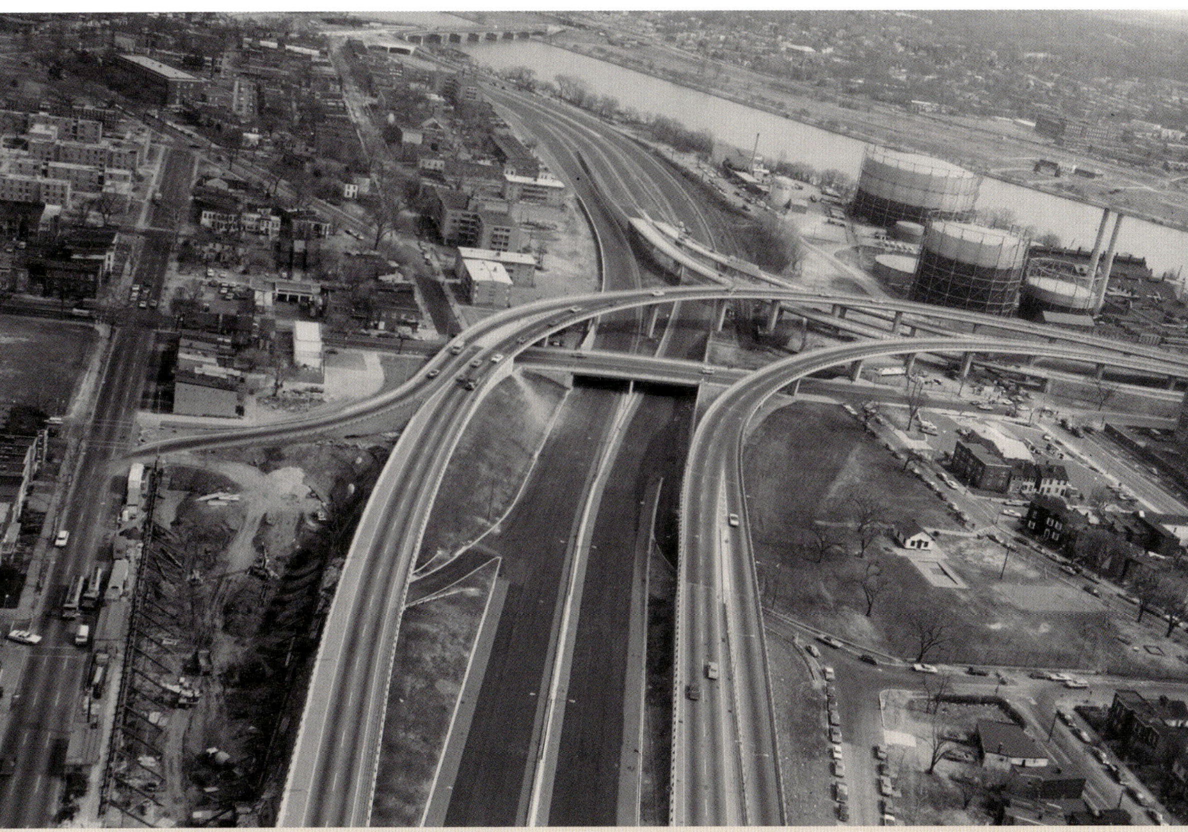

This 1973 photograph shows Interstate 695 from Thirteenth Street SE to the John Philip Sousa Bridge. Near the river are the Washington Gas Light gasometers (demolished). I Street is left of and parallel to the freeway. Along Potomac Avenue, the diagonal street at upper left, are Potomac Gardens and Chamberlain School. (Courtesy DC Department of Transportation.)

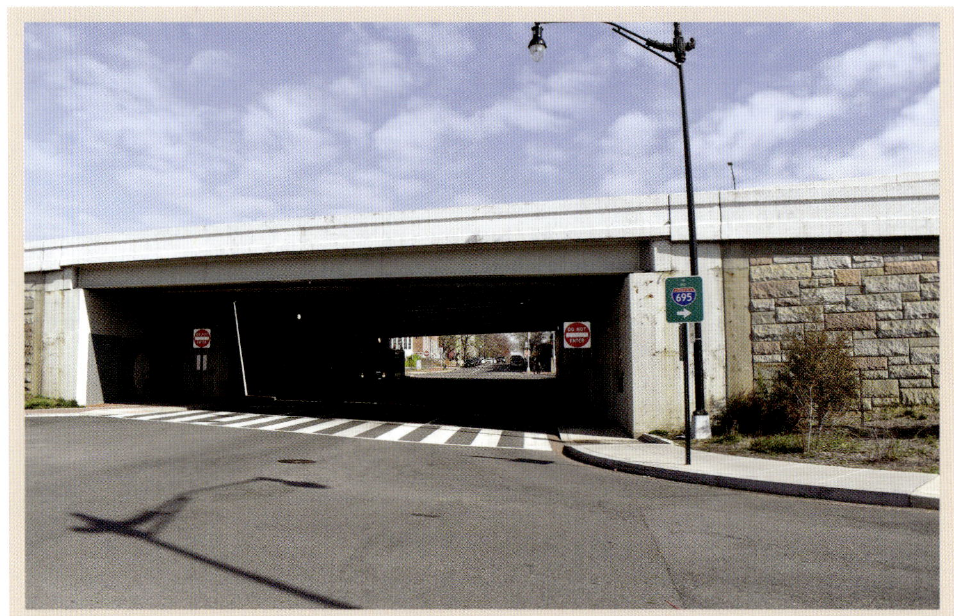

Founded in 1810, the Second Regular Baptist Church, originally known as the Baptist Church of the Navy Yard, built a series of buildings at Fourth Street and Virginia Avenue SE and moved in 1934. The Way of the Cross Church, founded in 1928, had grown quickly and, in 1935, bought the Baptist church. In 1963, that church sold the building for highway construction and moved to 819 D Street NE. (Photograph by Russell Jones; courtesy LOC, HABS DC, WASH-149.)

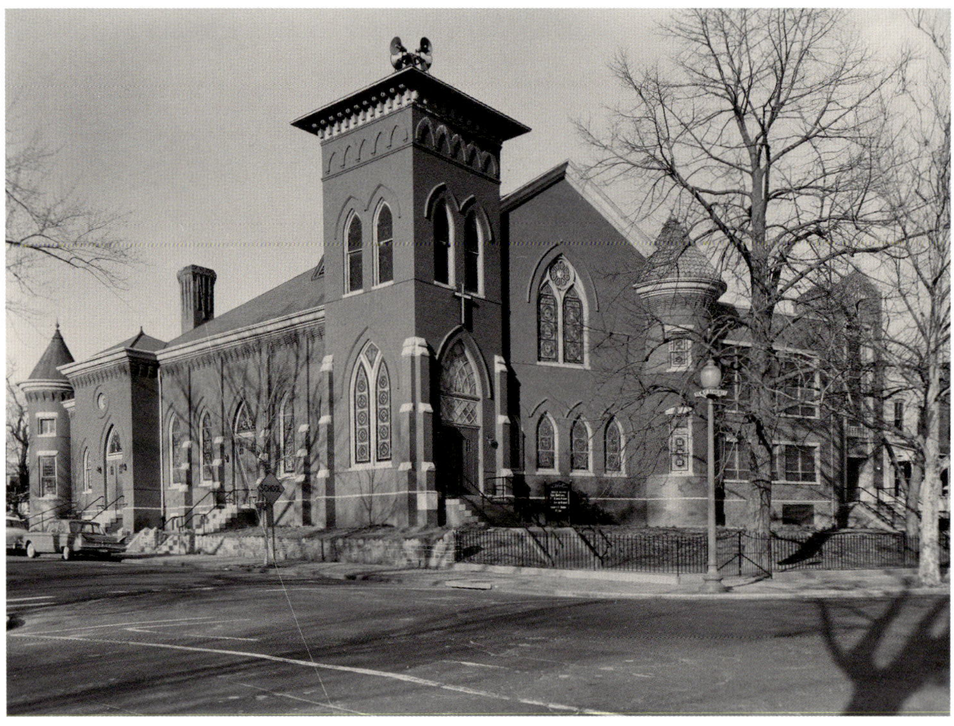

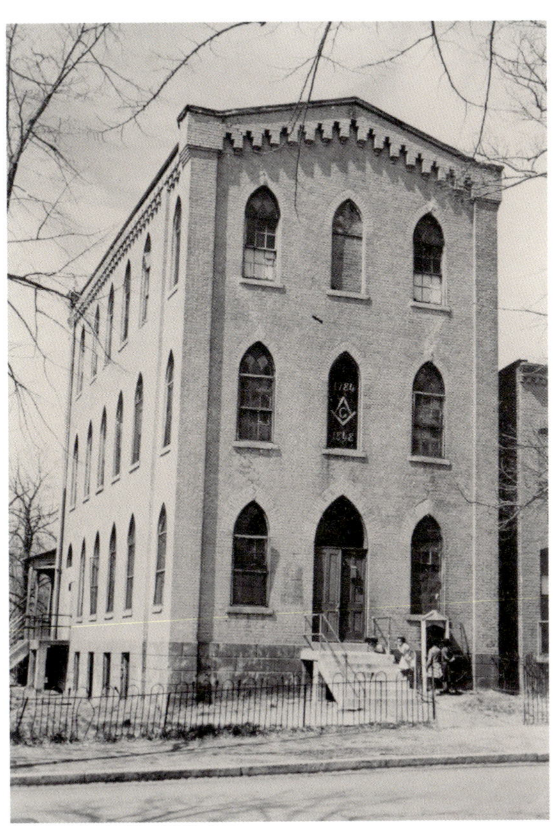

In 1821, Naval Lodge No. 4 built its lodge, a 19th-century Gothic vernacular building, the city's earliest nonecclesiastical building of this type, at Fifth Street and Virginia Avenue SE. Members added a third story in 1867. Naval Lodge No. 4 moved to 330 Pennsylvania Avenue SE in 1895. African American Masons and a Baptist church later used the original building. The building was demolished in the 1960s for highway construction. (Photograph by Russell Jones; courtesy LOC, HABS DCWASH-149.)

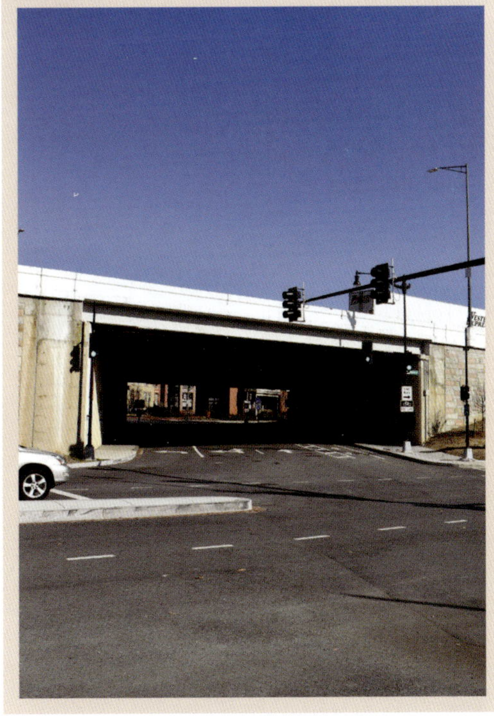

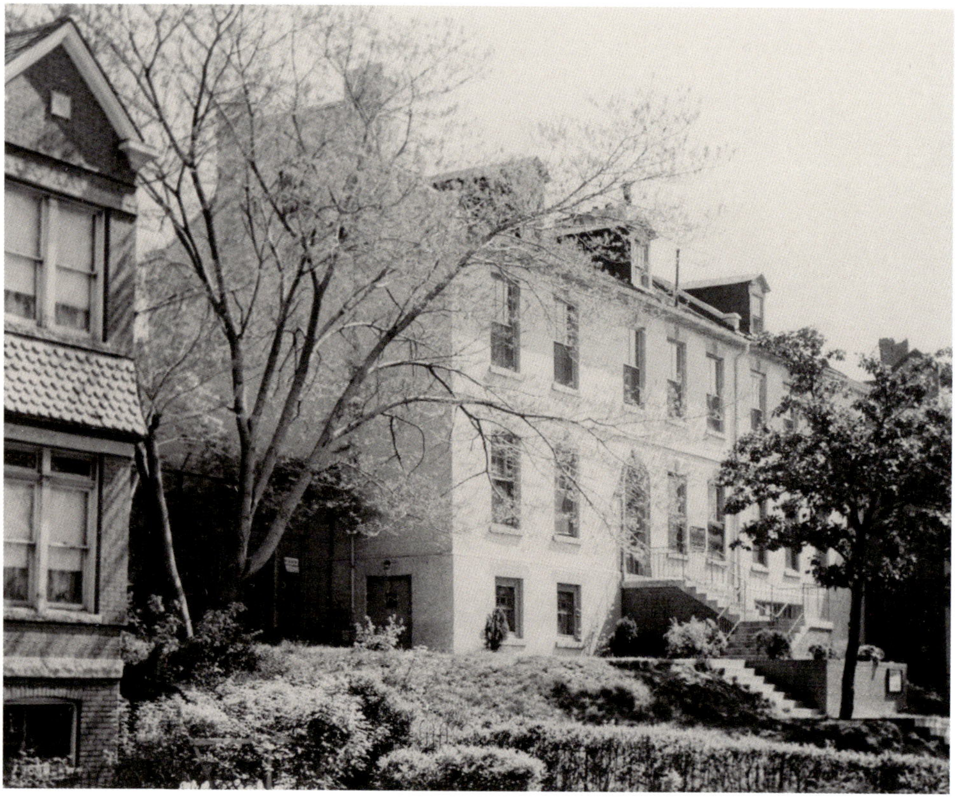

The two-story brick row houses with dormers at 324–326 Virginia Avenue SE were built in the early 19th century. Samuel N. Smallwood (1772–1824), twice the mayor of Washington, lived at 324. He provided the rock for the White House's foundations and supervised enslaved people who built the Capitol. The past photograph is from 1959. These houses were demolished in the 1960s for the Southeast–Southwest Freeway (Interstate 695). (Photograph by Russell Jones; courtesy LOC, HABS DCWASH-149.)

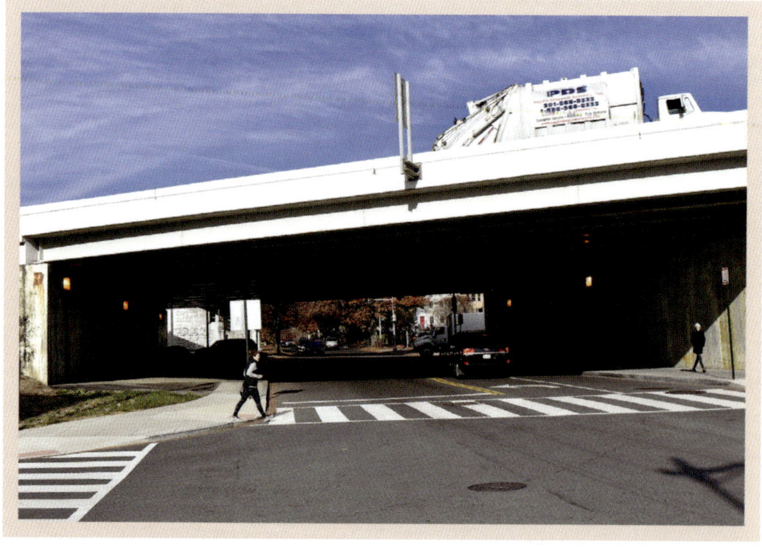

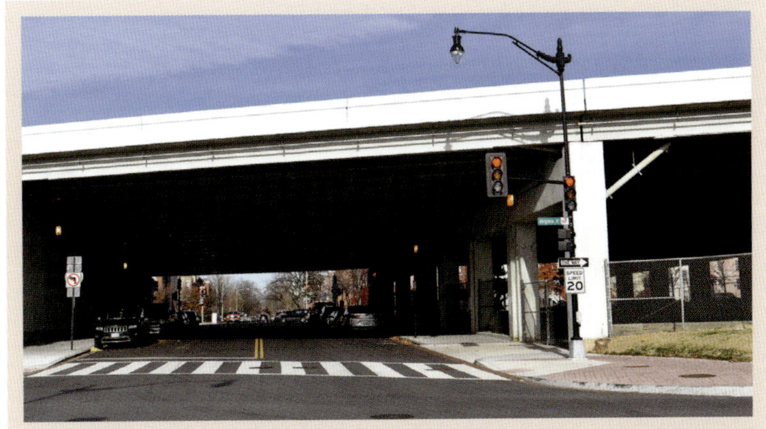

In 1895, Mary Dougherty built a family home at 725 Virginia Avenue SE, and in 1900, added rental houses at 716–722 Virginia Avenue SE. Mary Agnes Dougherty inherited them in 1929 and continued to rent to Navy Yard workers and others until she died in 1951. Not long after this 1966 photograph, all houses were demolished for the Southeast–Southwest Freeway. (Photograph by William E. Barrett; courtesy Historical Society of Washington, DC, KC-2179.)

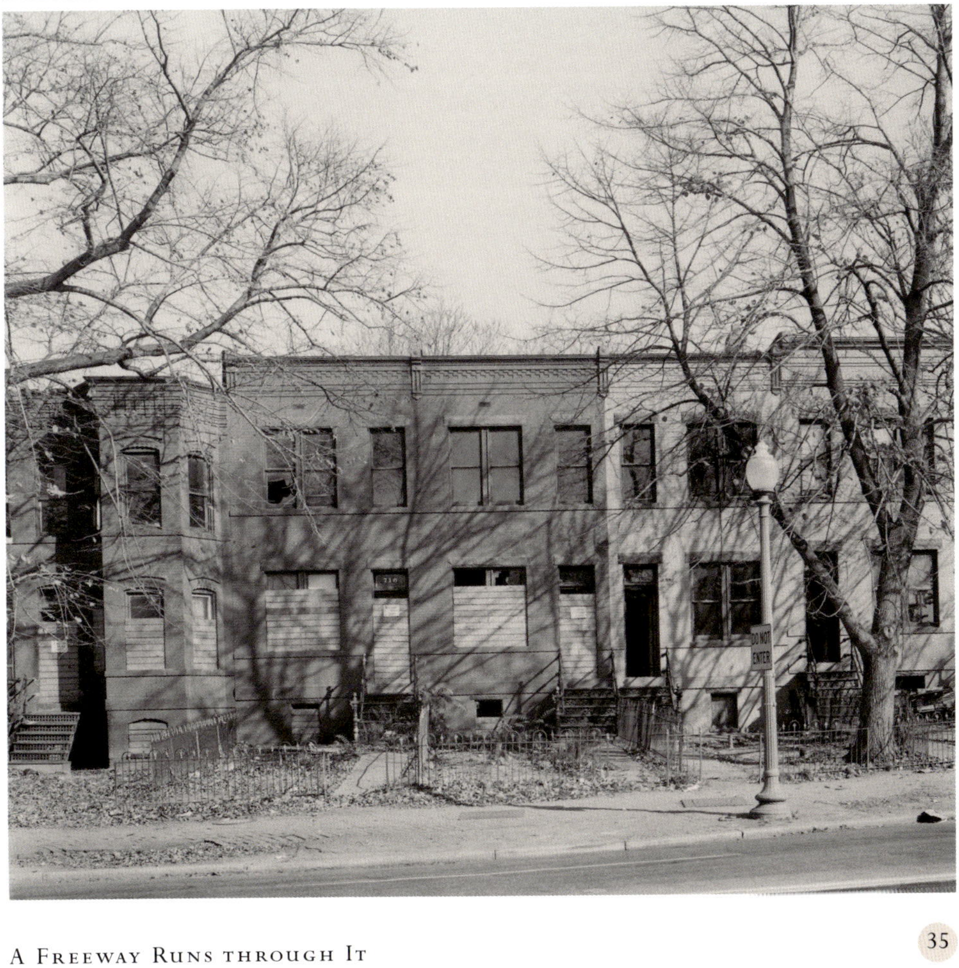

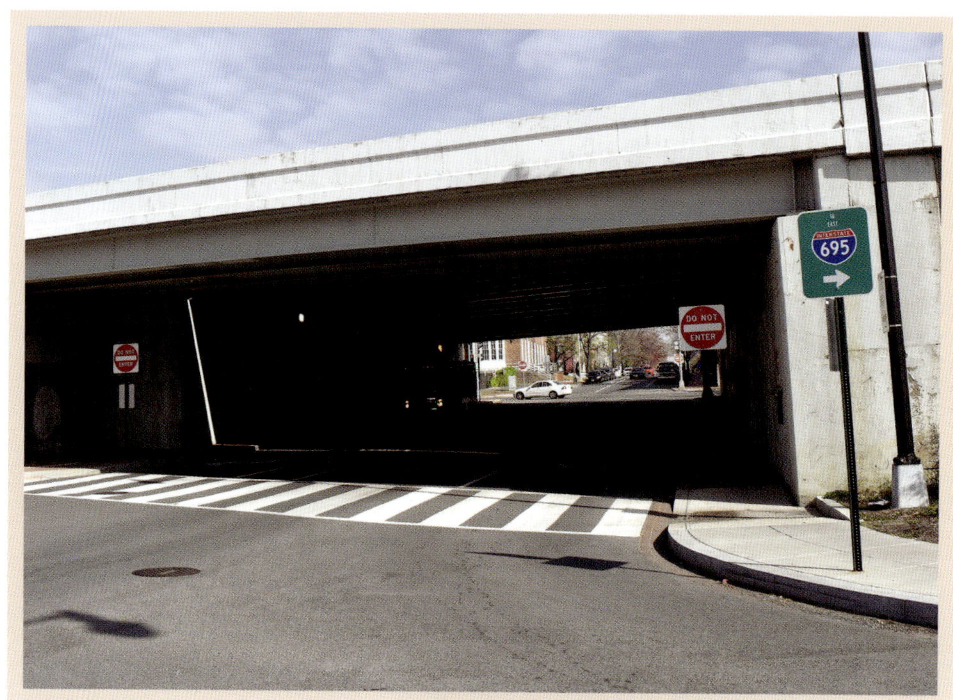

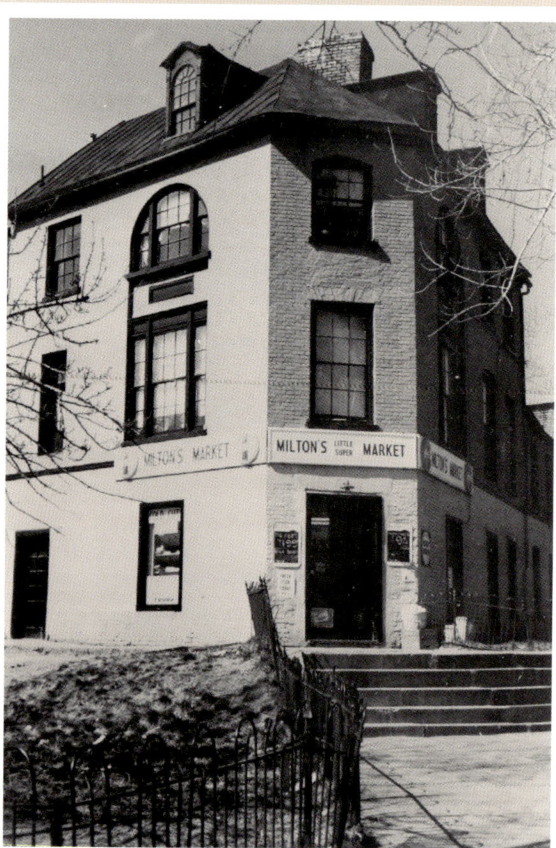

The three-story brick building with a canted entrance at 330 Virginia Avenue SE was built in the 19th century. Charles Hawkins operated his drugstore here from about 1901 to 1923. Milton A. Wilson Sr. (1893–1965), an African American, lived here with his family and operated Milton's Market from approximately 1935 to approximately 1959. The building was demolished in the 1960s to build the freeway. (Photograph by Russell Jones; courtesy LOC, HABS DCWASH-149.)

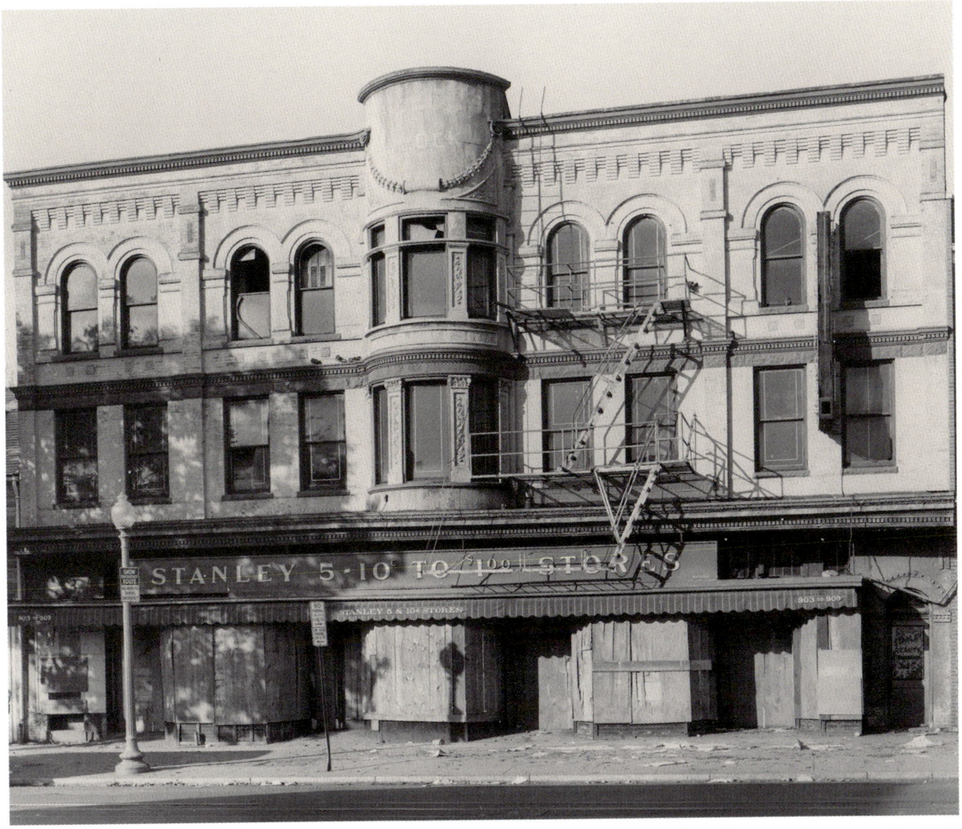

Stanley 5–10¢ to $1.00 Stores operated at 903–909 Eighth Street SE and was razed in the 1960s to build the Southeast–Southwest Freeway. The store's site is now beneath the freeway overpass on Eighth Street SE (also known as Barracks Row). (Photograph by William E. Barrett; courtesy Historical Society of Washington, DC, KC-2157.)

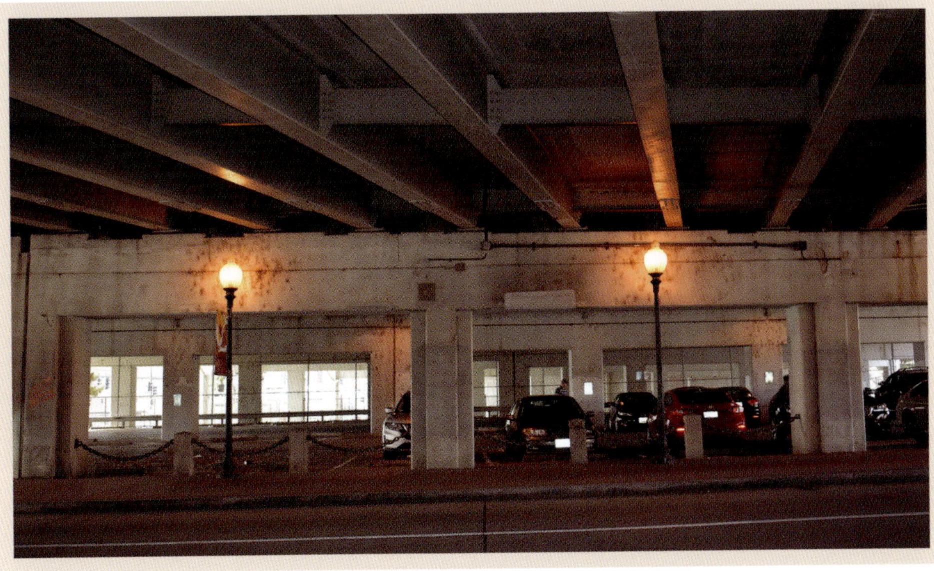

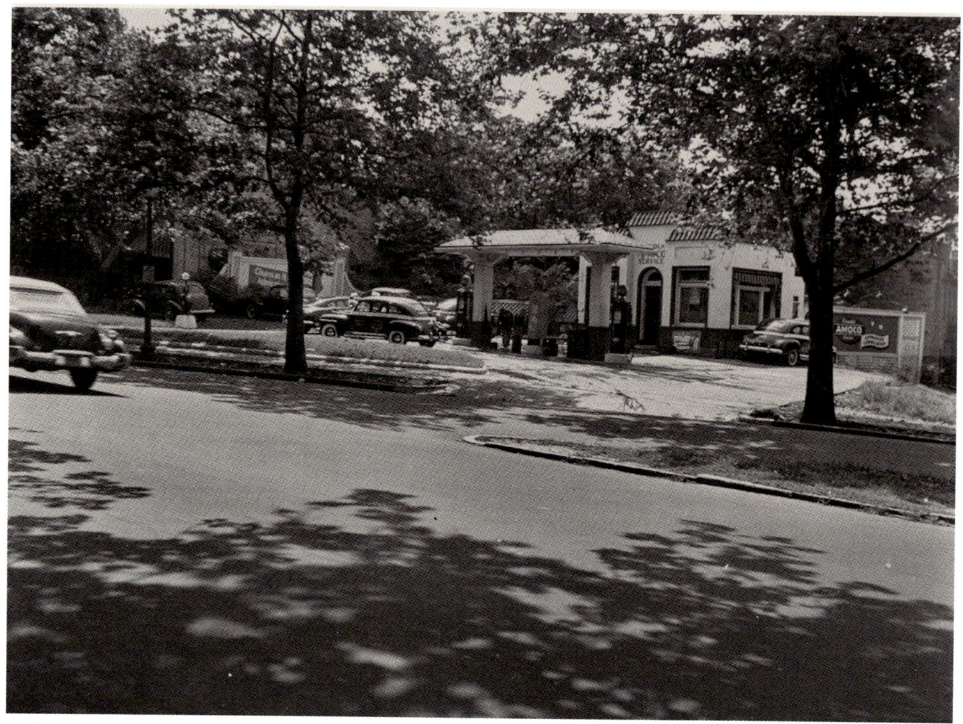

Lincoln Amoco Service at 701 Virginia Avenue SE, seen here in 1949, had decorative elements used in many period stations; in this case, a Mediterranean tile roof and also a drive-through, a feature introduced by Amoco. The station was demolished for highway construction. (Photograph by John P. Wymer; courtesy Historical Society of Washington, DC, WY-1507.)

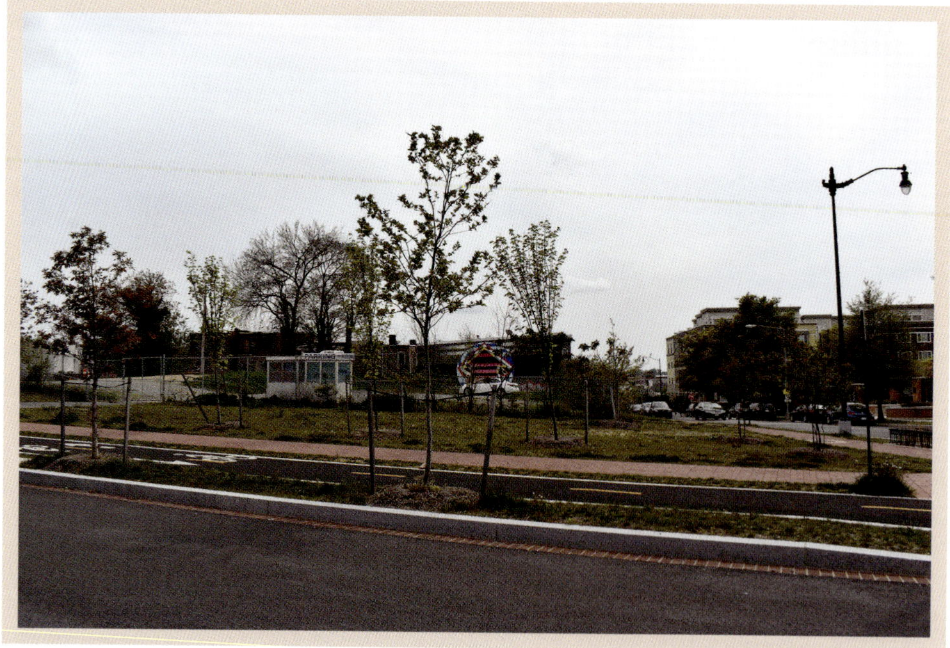

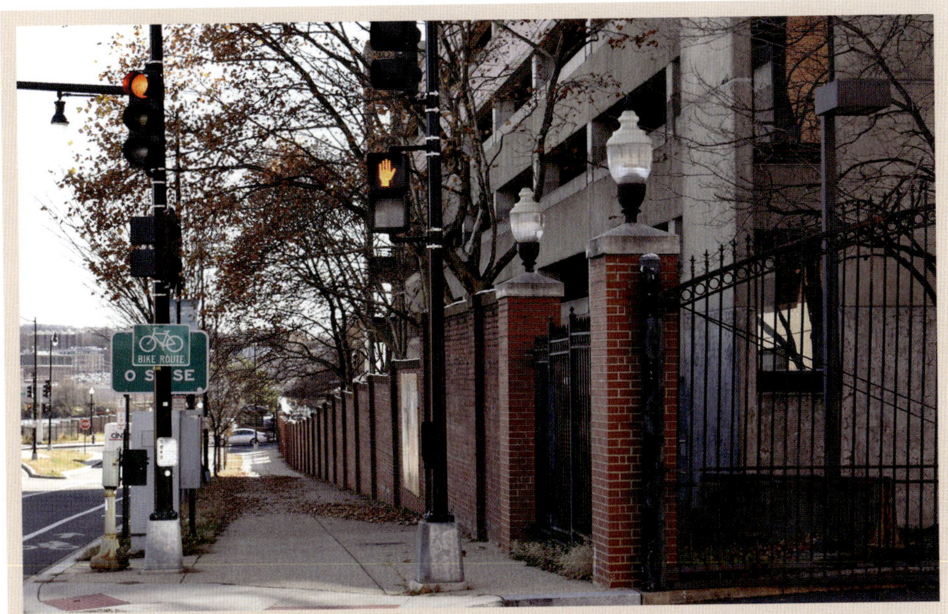

These auto repair businesses at Eleventh and N Streets SE were near the Washington Gas Light gasometers and the Anacostia River and east of the Washington Navy Yard. While industrial uses would be expected so near the gasometers, people also lived on Eleventh Street, and the Port Hole Grill (not pictured) was at 1336 Eleventh Street. Freeway ramps now cover the area. (Photograph by John P. Wymer; courtesy Historical Society of Washington, DC, WY-3527.)

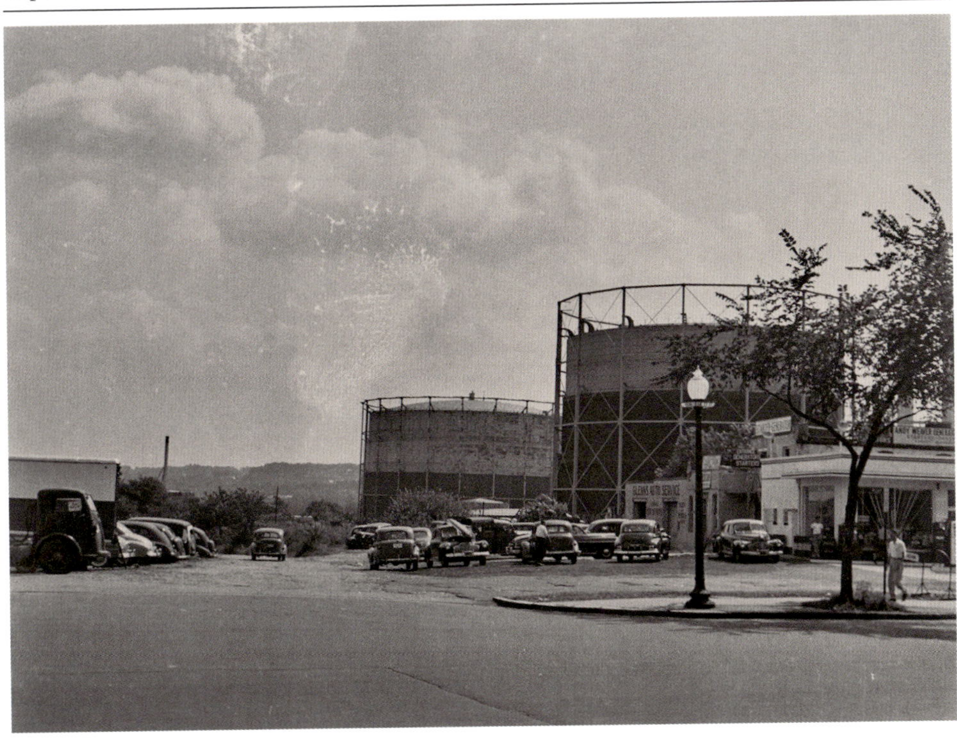

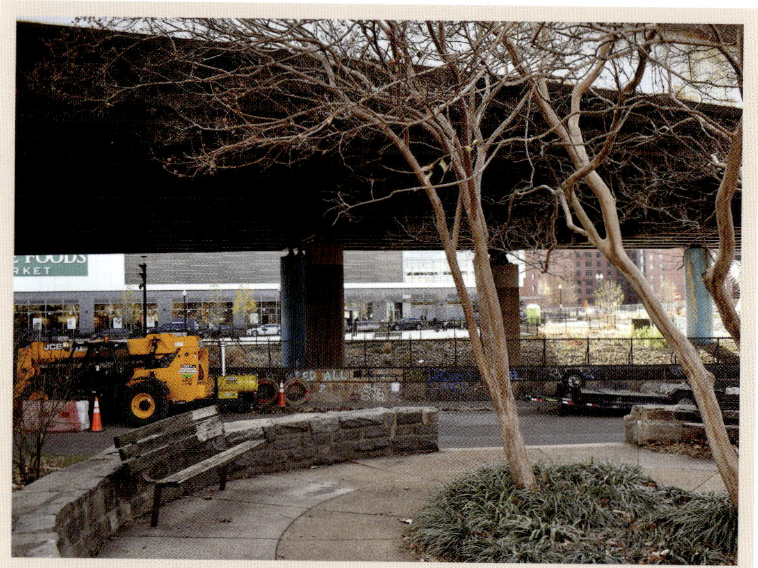

Garfield Park, between New Jersey Avenue and Third Street SE, has been a park since the 19th century. Neighbors recall visiting the park house in the 1950s and 1960s for arts and crafts and swimming in the nearby pool. While the park house survived freeway construction, it was later disassembled and moved, it is believed, to Rock Creek Park. Today, Whole Foods at 101 H Street SE is visible south of the freeway. (Courtesy DC Department of Transportation.)

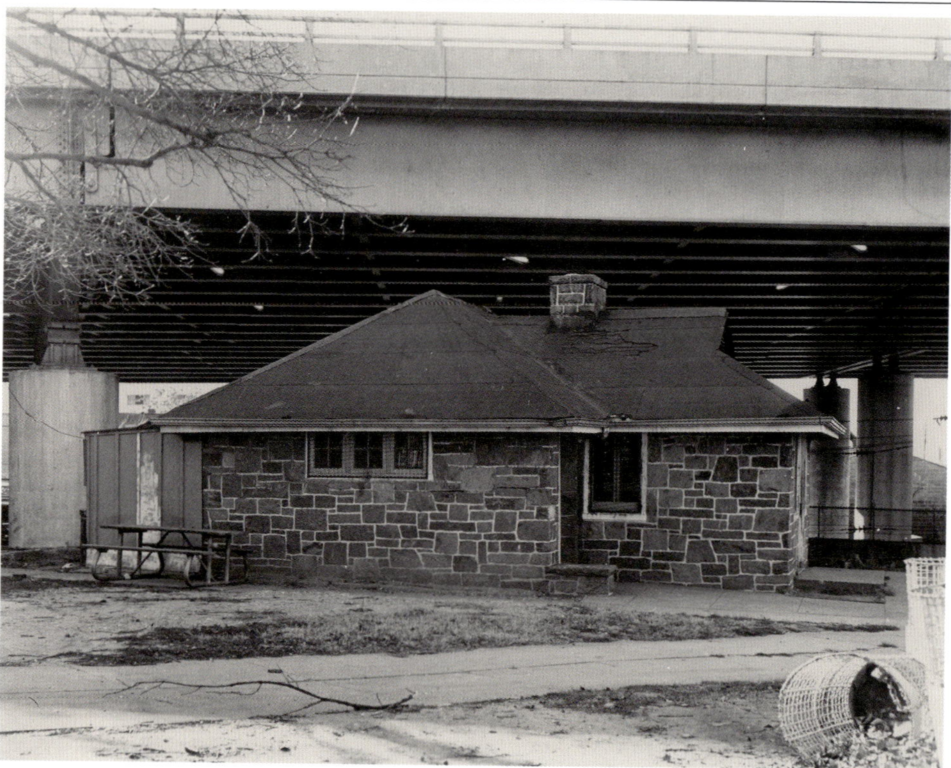

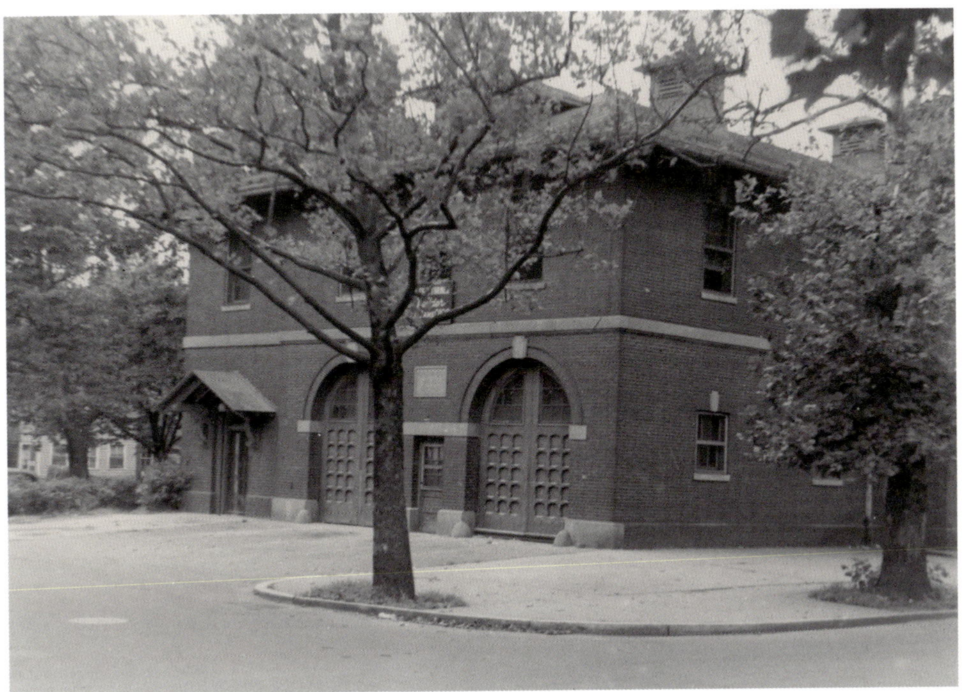

Reservation 124A at the intersection of Virginia and Georgia (now Potomac) Avenues was originally reserved for public use. The Anacostia Fire Company building, which was also used as the Anacostia Public School, was located here between 1857 and 1870. Engine Company No. 18's station, photographed in 1949, was demolished for the Southeast–Southwest Freeway. (Photograph by John P. Wymer; courtesy Historical Society of Washington, DC, WY-1495.)

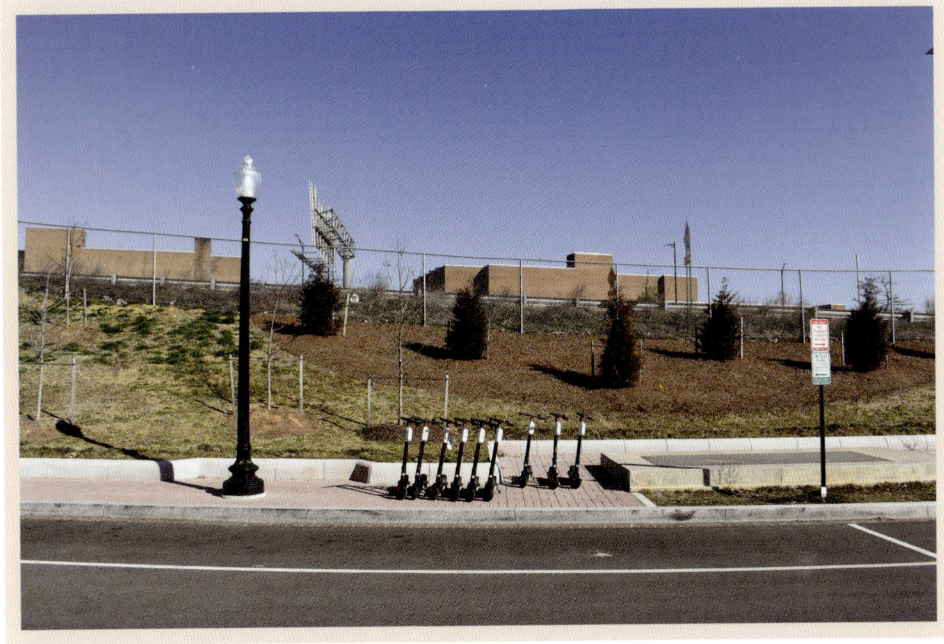

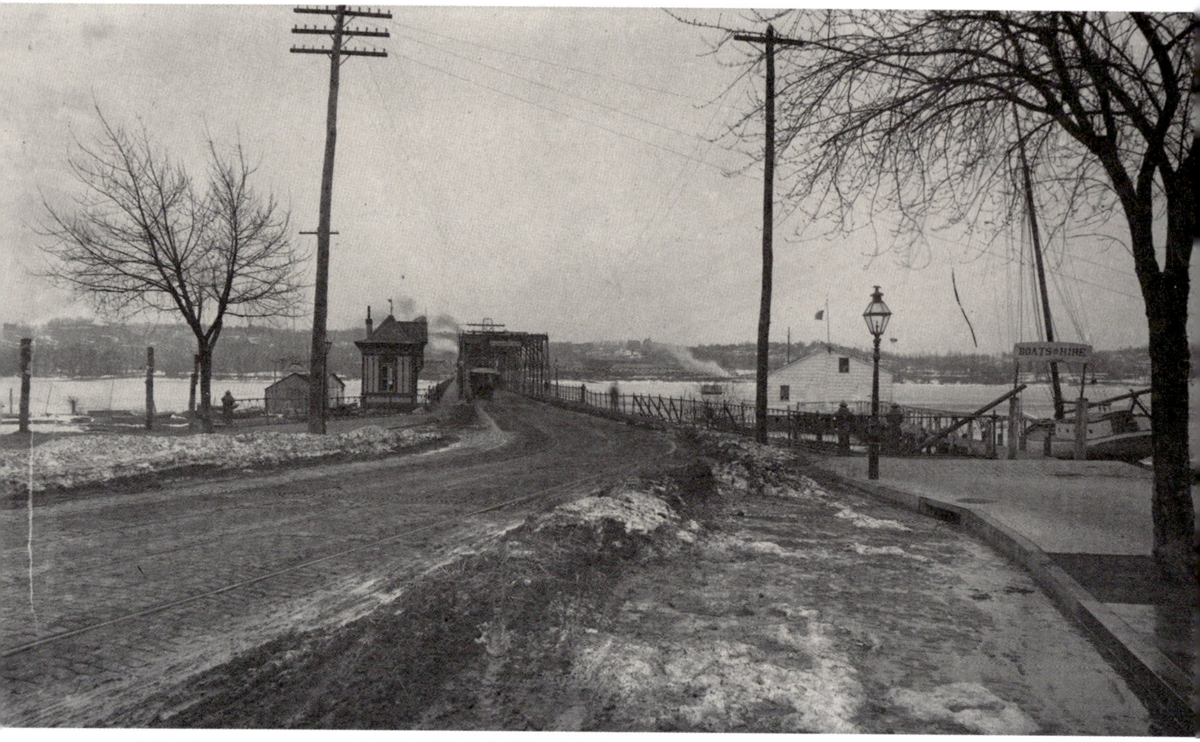

After John Wilkes Booth shot President Lincoln on April 14, 1865, he rode to the Navy Yard Bridge, where the guard allowed him cross to Uniontown (now Anacostia). He then rode into Maryland. The bridge, built in 1818, was replaced by an iron truss bridge in 1883, shown in this photograph around 1893. In the 1960s, a highway bridge was built here, which was replaced again in the 2010s. (Courtesy Historical Society of Washington, DC, CHS-06805.)

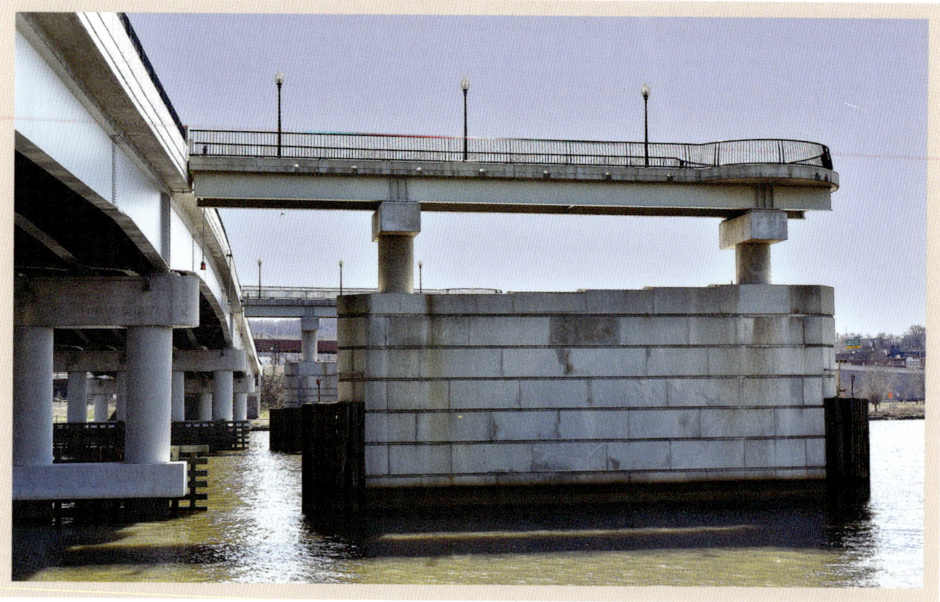

CHAPTER 4

Higher and Better Uses

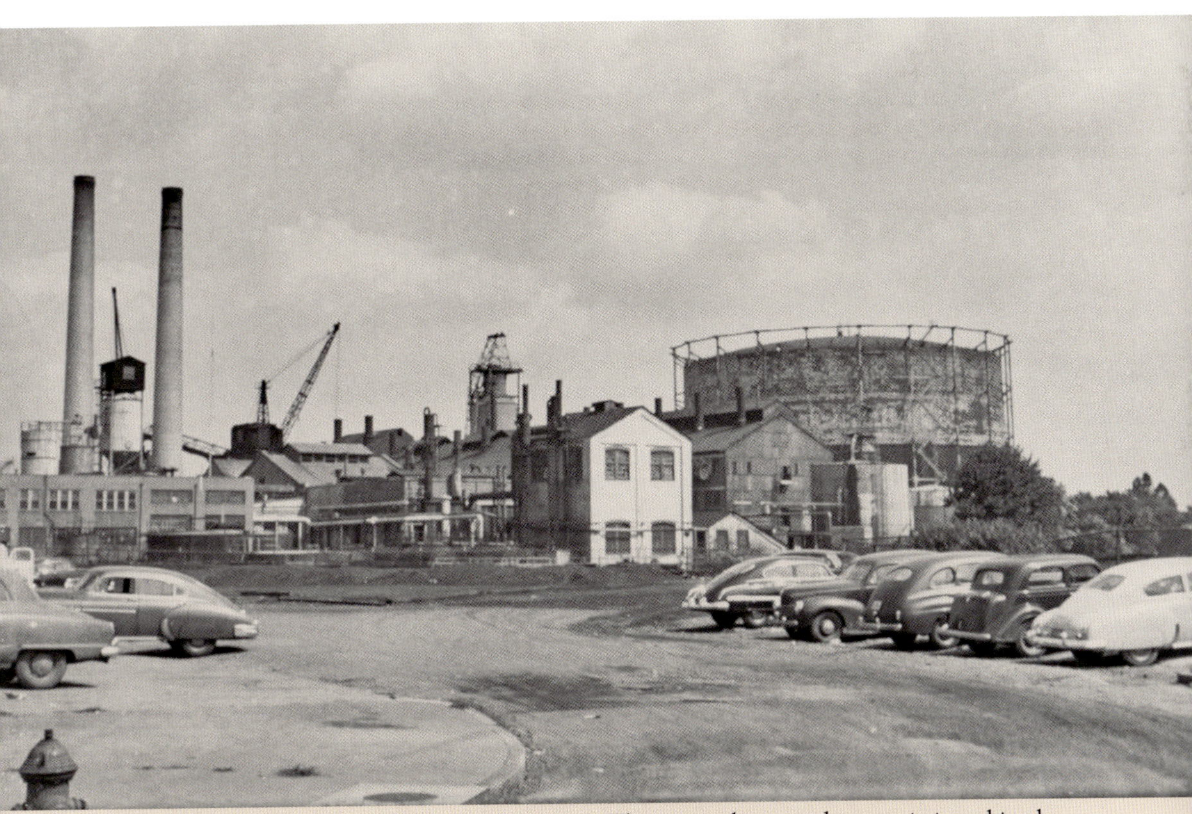

Washington Gas Light Company built gas station works in the city, first in Foggy Bottom in 1858 and the East Station Gasworks on the Anacostia River in 1888, seen here in 1950. The cylindrical gasometers stored gas. The gasworks were decommissioned in the 1990s. (Photograph by John P. Wymer; courtesy Historical Society of Washington, DC, WY-3528.)

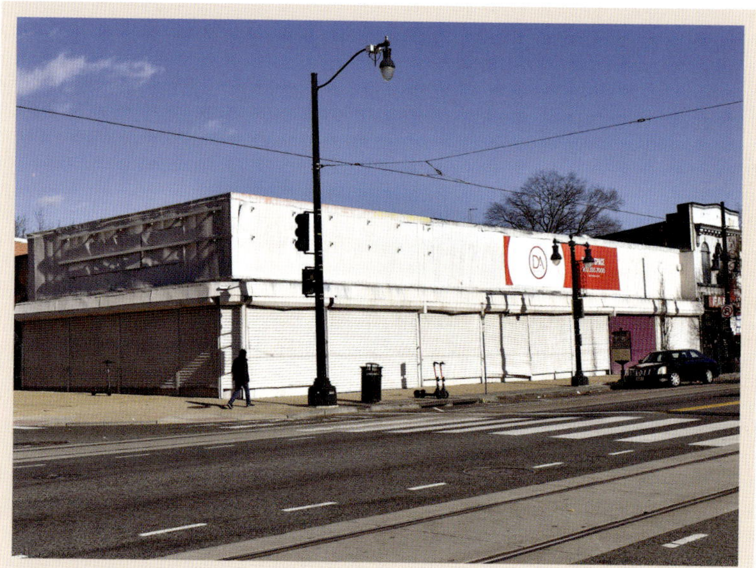

Gustavus Blechman (1872–1965), a Jewish immigrant from Russia, operated a clothing store for men and women for 50 years at 700 H Street NE, ending in 1948. It is shown around 1920. He advertised it as the "Northeast's Big Bargain Corner." For a time, his family lived above the store. Blechman's sons owned McBride's Department Store, and in 1948, they demolished the old building and replaced it with a one-story building for McBride's. (Courtesy LOC, FC-F82-5612.)

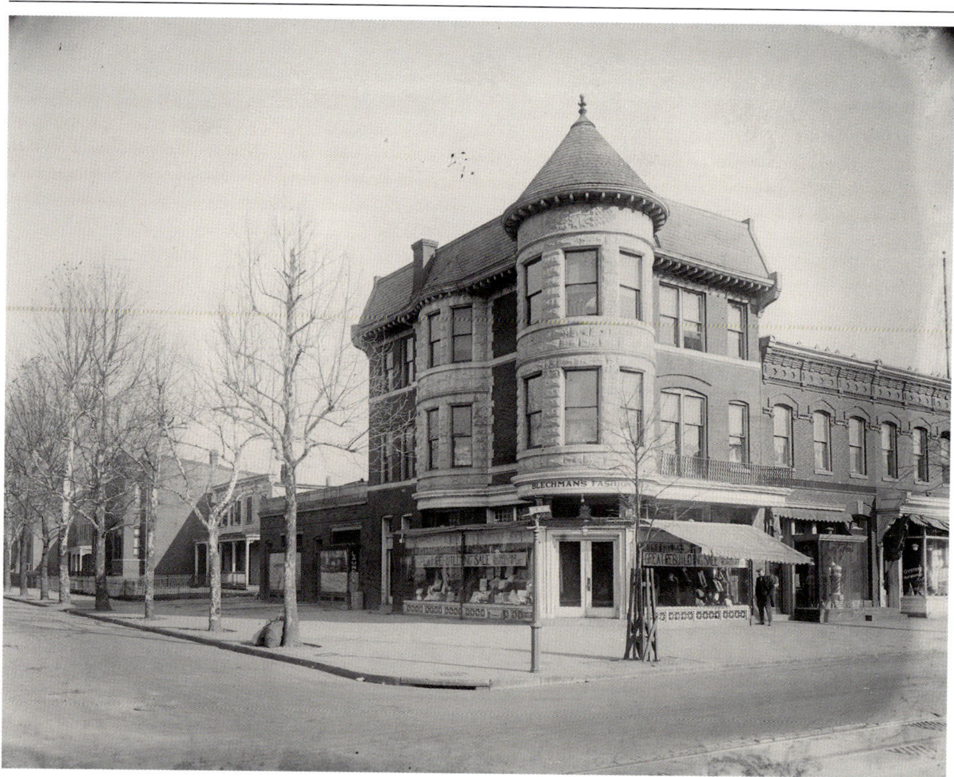

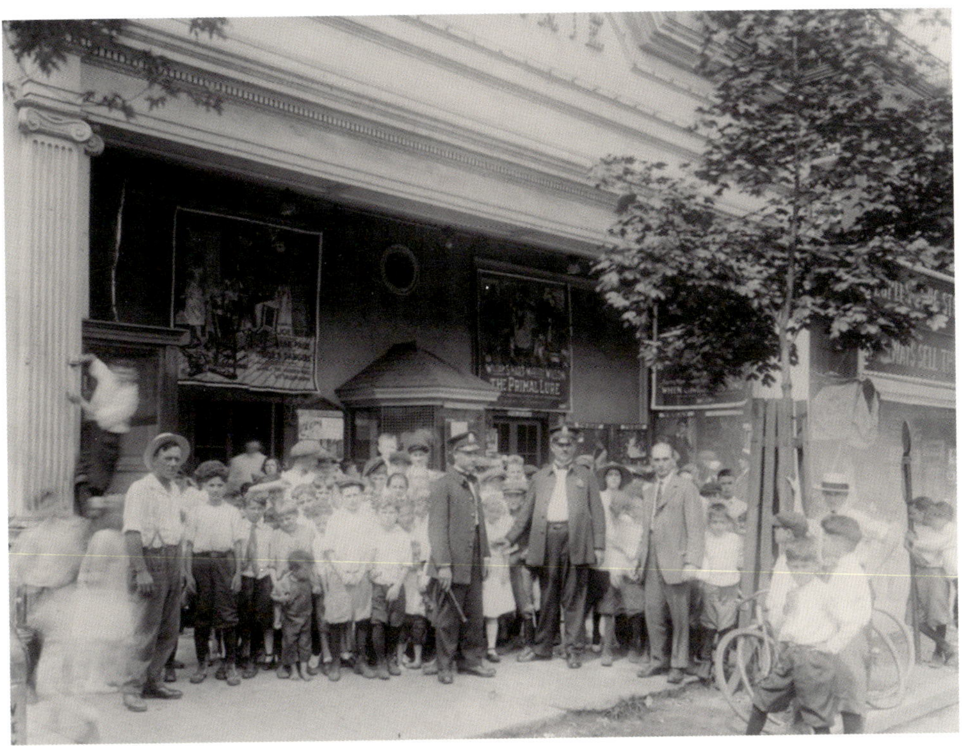

The Dixie Theater at 800 H Street NE, shown around 1920, was designed by Clark Jones and Seward Charles. Seating almost 400, it opened in 1910 and was popular with children. *The Primal Lure*, a 1916 silent Western starring William S. Hart, was playing. The theater was demolished in 1921 to build the Northeast Savings Bank (now a PNC Bank branch), designed by B. Stanley Simmons. (Courtesy LOC, LOT 12342-10.)

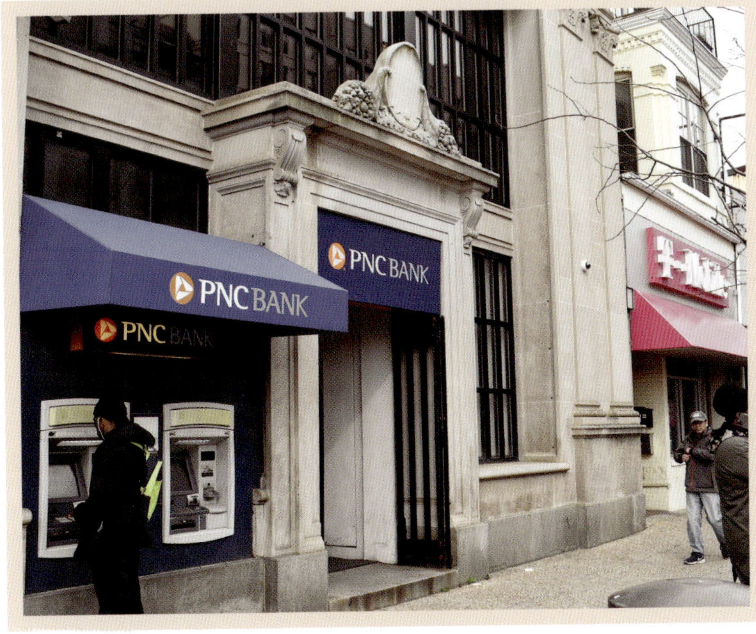

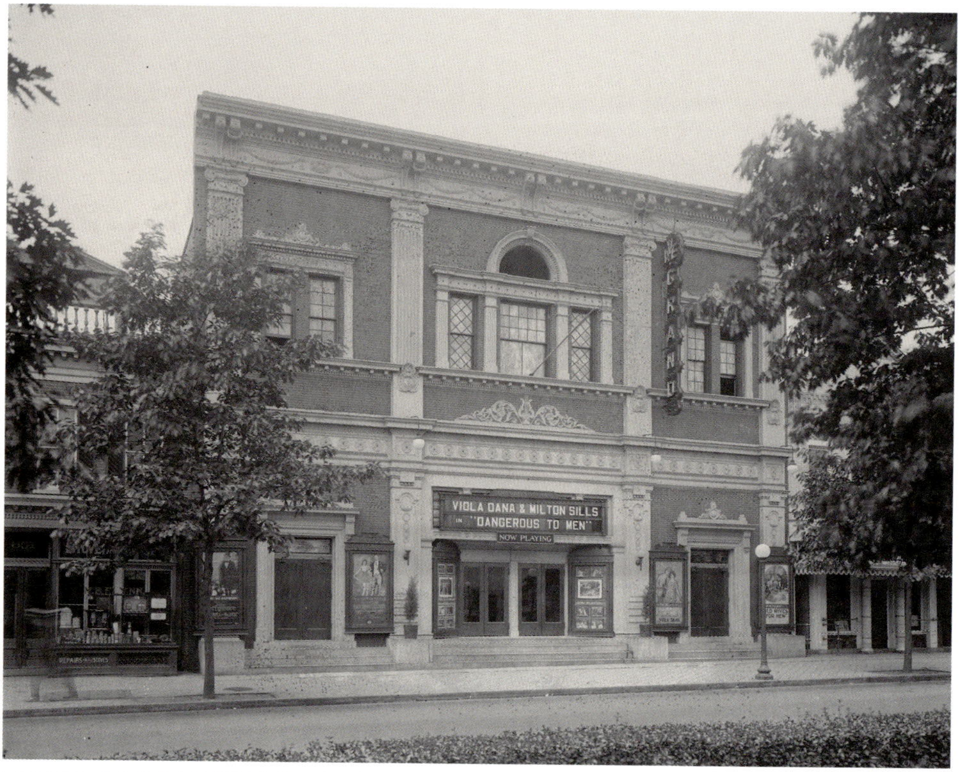

In 1910, William C. Allard designed the Classical Revival–style Avenue Grand at 645 Pennsylvania Avenue SE in pressed brick with garlands at the cornice and Ionic pilasters, seen around 1920. Appleton P. Clark remodeled it in 1916. It seated 840 to 1,100 people. One of the longest-surviving theaters, it lasted until 1970, when it burned. It was replaced by a commercial building in 1980. (Courtesy LOC, LC-F82-4361.)

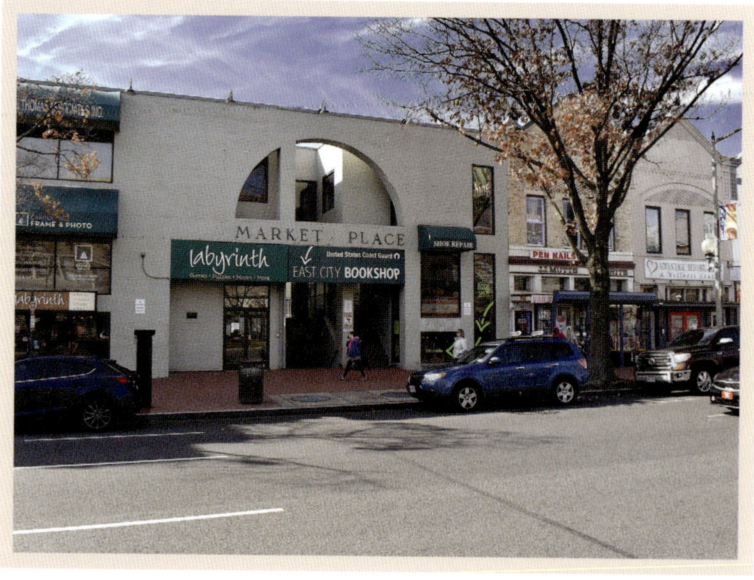

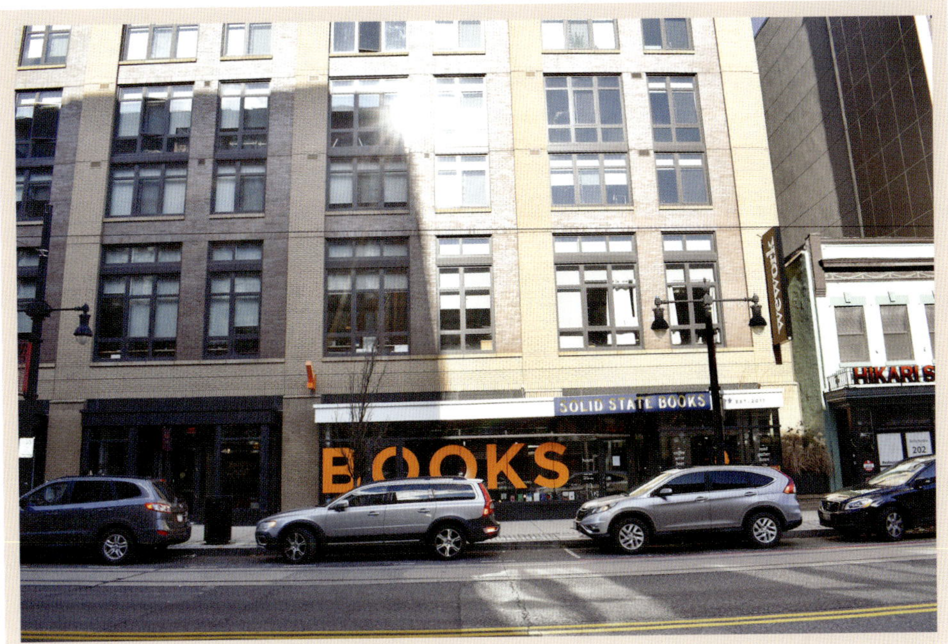

The Apollo Theatre at 624 H Street NE, designed by C. Clark James and built in 1913, seated 800 and attracted customers with 70 incandescent lights in a black-white-and-gold sign. *Fedora*, a silent drama starring Pauline Frederick, and *Money Mad*, a silent mystery starring Mae Marsh, were playing around 1918. It closed in 1955. The Apollo, a large multiuse project built in 2016, now occupies the site. (Courtesy LOC, LC-F82-2281.)

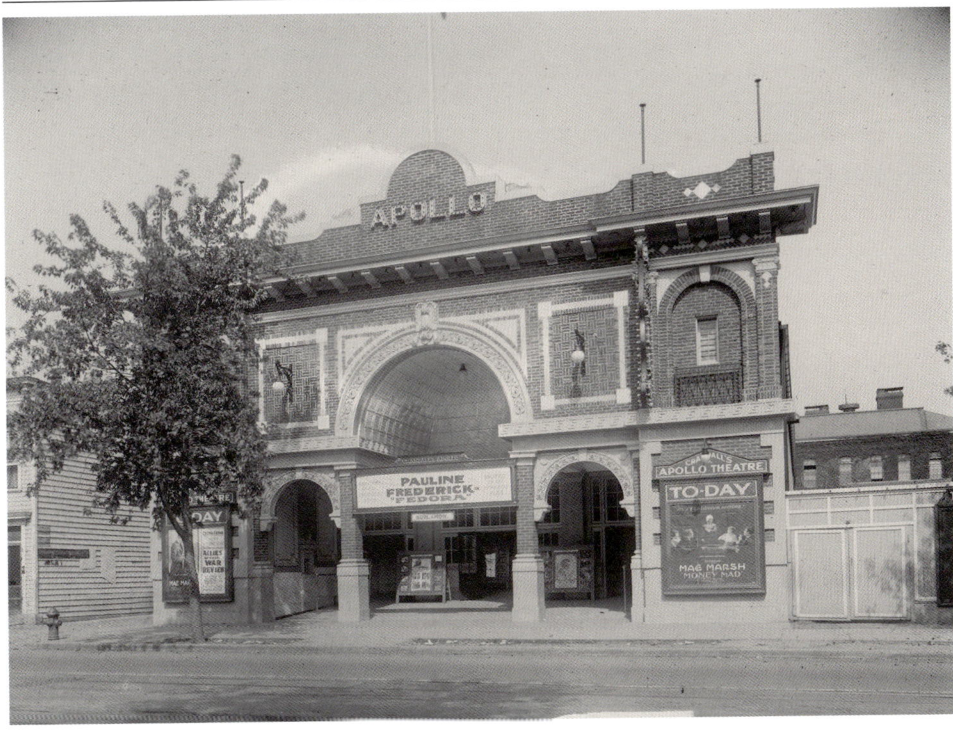

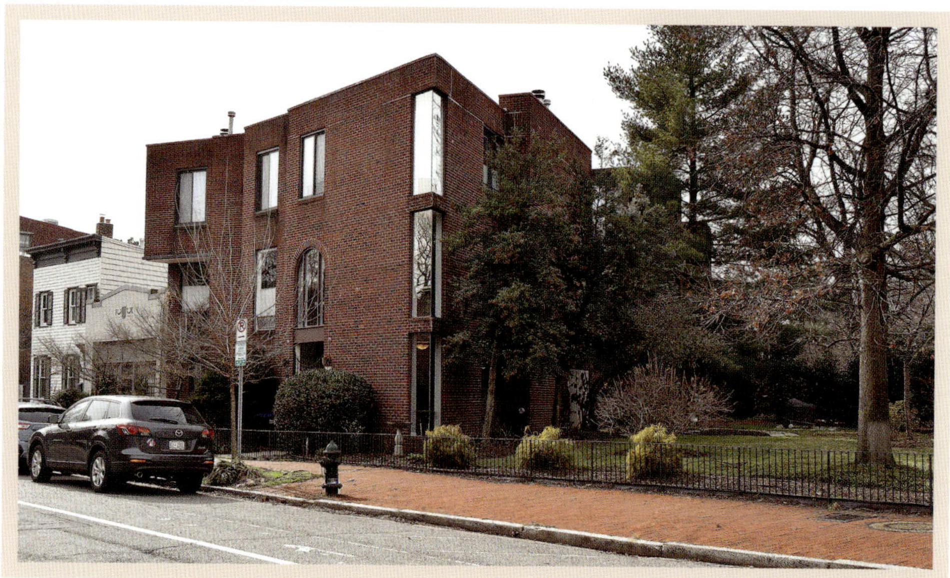

The Carolina Theater at 105 Eleventh Street SE opened in 1913. B.F. Myers designed the building; William S. Plager redesigned and expanded the seating in 1919. Shown in 1949, it had stores on either side. It closed in 1952 and was demolished in the 1970s. Palace Laundry, at 111 Eleventh Street, and 109 Eleventh Street SE are now residential. The Lincoln Park West Condominiums were built here in 1980. (Photograph by John P. Wymer; courtesy Historical Society of Washington, DC, WY-1478.)

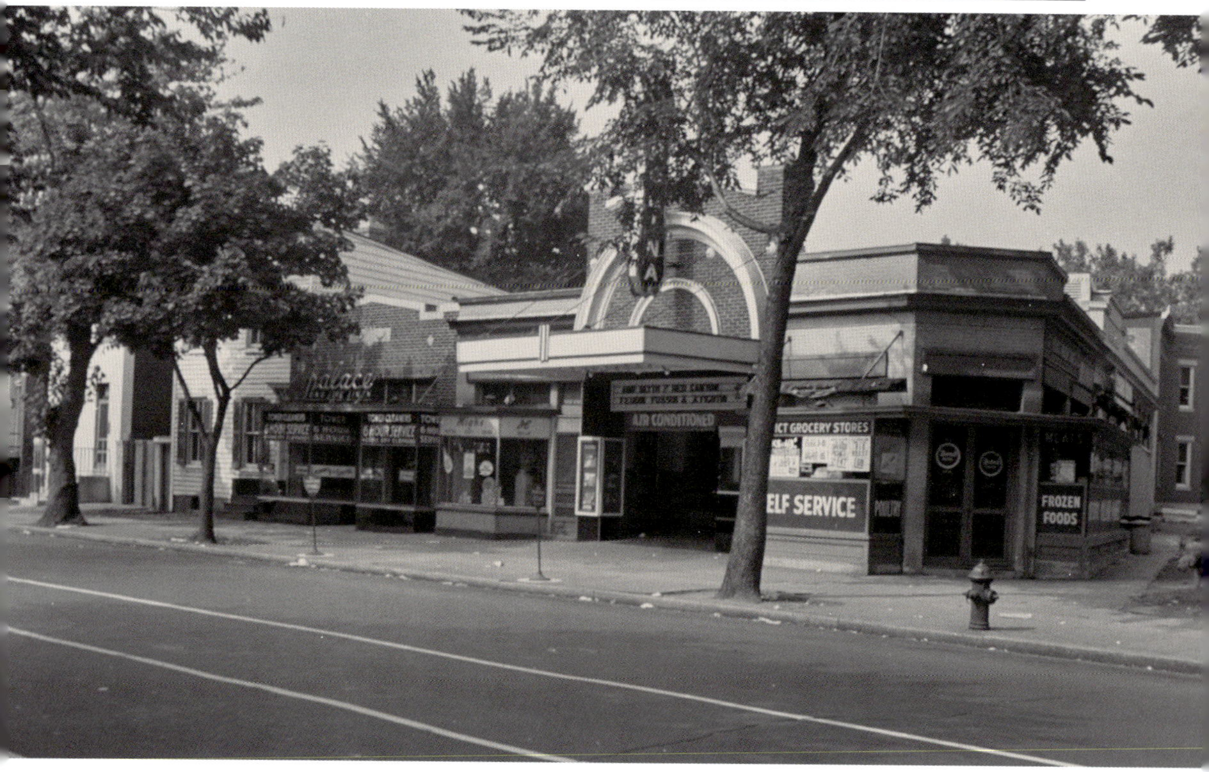

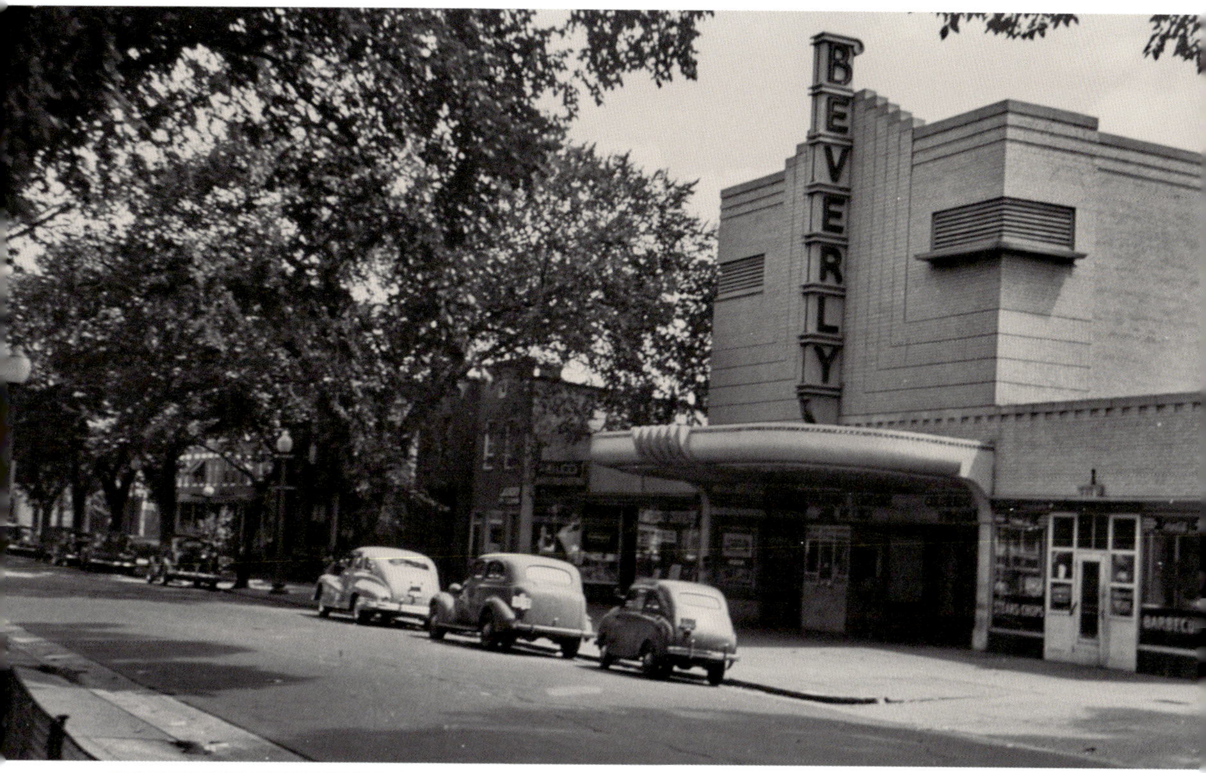

In 1939, Warner Bros. built the Art Deco Beverly Theater at 511–519 Fifteenth Street NE to compete with the Atlas Theater, at 1331 H Street NE, which opened in 1938. John Eberson designed the theater. In 1949, *Colorado Territory*, starring Joel McCrae and Virginia Mayo, was playing. The theater was demolished in 1963 for parking at Miner Elementary School. (Photograph by John P. Wymer; courtesy Historical Society of Washington, DC, WY-1304.)

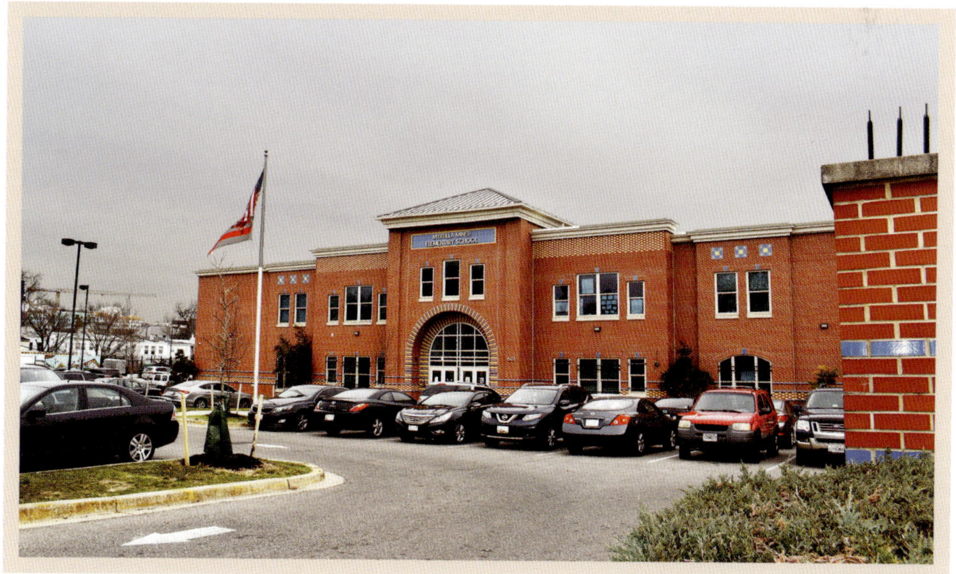

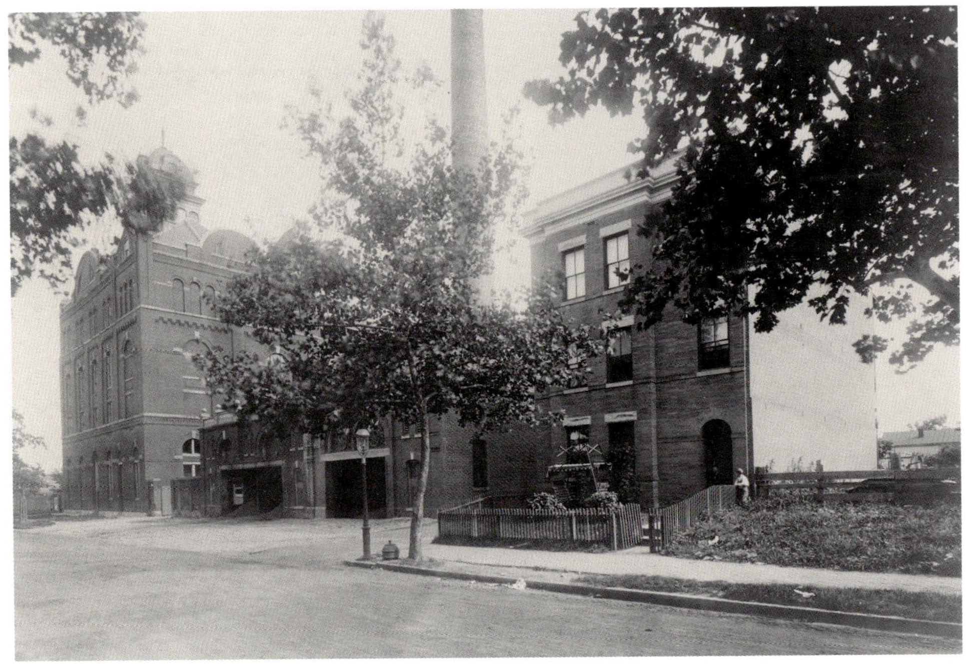

Beer was brewed in Square 1042 (Thirteenth/Fourteenth/D/E Streets SE) from 1850 to 1917. Albert Cary and Robert Portner bought the brewery in 1890, renaming it the National Capital Brewing Company, and built a five-story brewhouse. With Prohibition, Meadowgold Dairy repurposed the brewery. The dairy was replaced by Safeway in 1962 and then by Beuchert's Park, a mixed-use project, in 2020. The "brewmaster's house" at 1331 D Street SE (1899) survives. (Courtesy LOC, LOT 123659-6.)

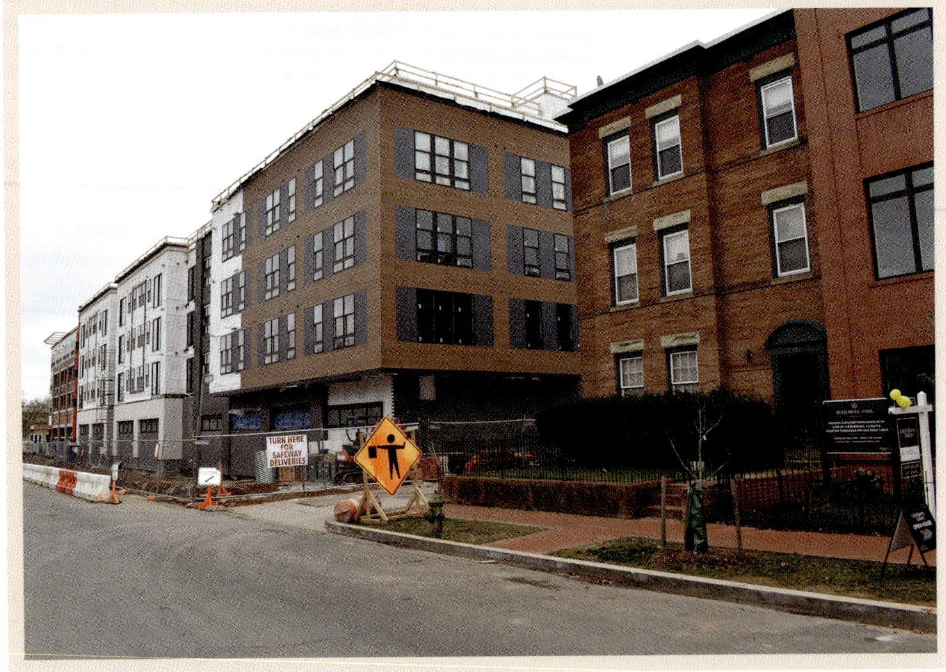

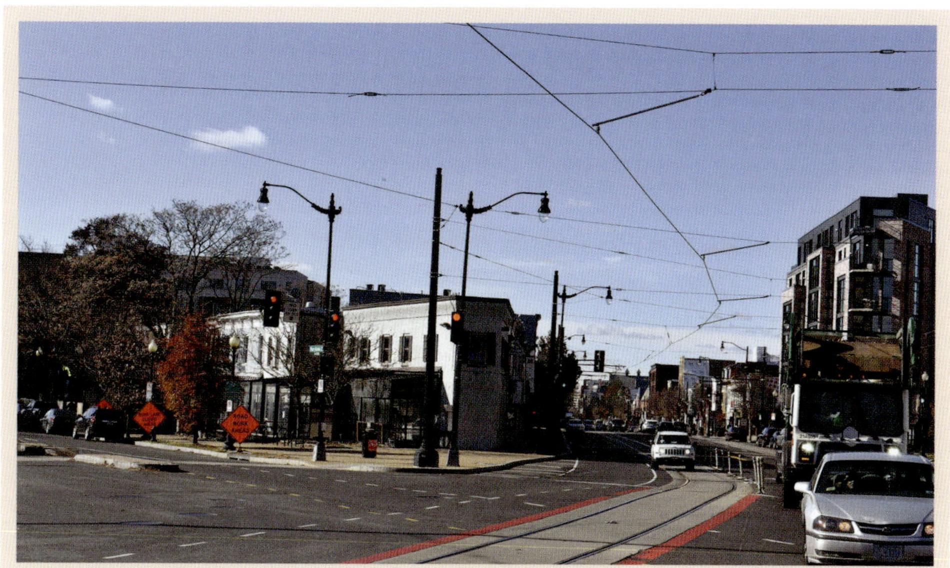

This 1950 photograph shows the intersection of H Street and Maryland Avenue NE. The two-story brick building at the apex was built in 1887 or earlier. The door has been moved. The Argonaut, a restaurant and bar, once operated at 1433 H Street. On the right in the present photograph is the Constellation on H Street, a mixed-use building at 1402 H Street NE, constructed in 2018. (Courtesy Historical Society of Washington, DC, WY-1283.)

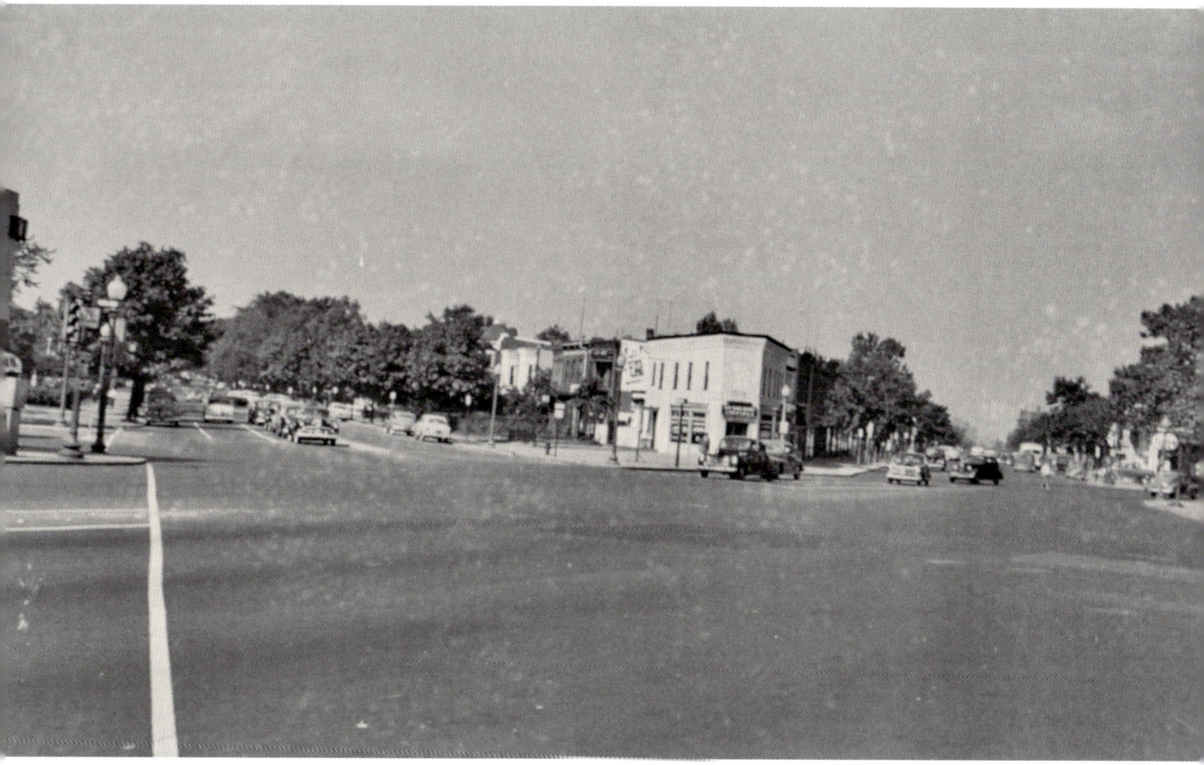

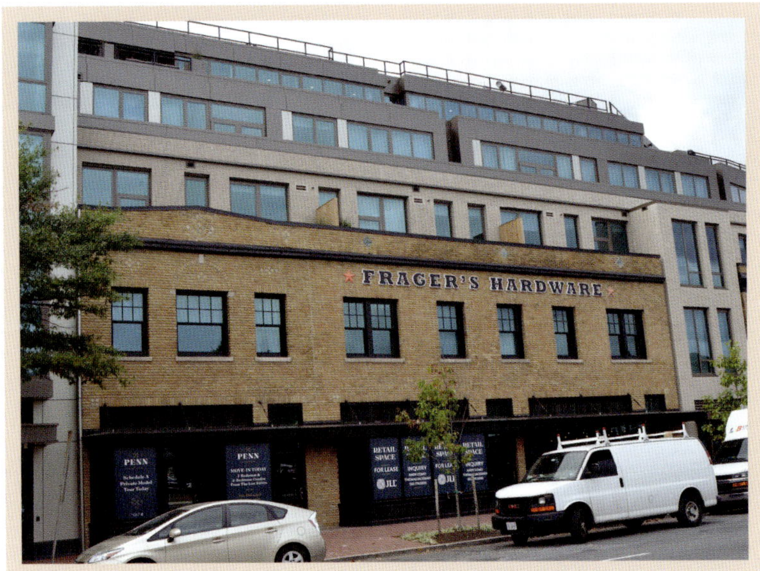

Frager's Hardware, designed by Julius Wenig, opened in 1920 at 1115 Pennsylvania Avenue SE and became a beloved community institution. When the store was seriously damaged by fire in 2013, neighbors rallied to support rebuilding. Three new residential stories were added to the building, wedding cake style, and Frager's Hardware reopened in 2019. (Author's collection.)

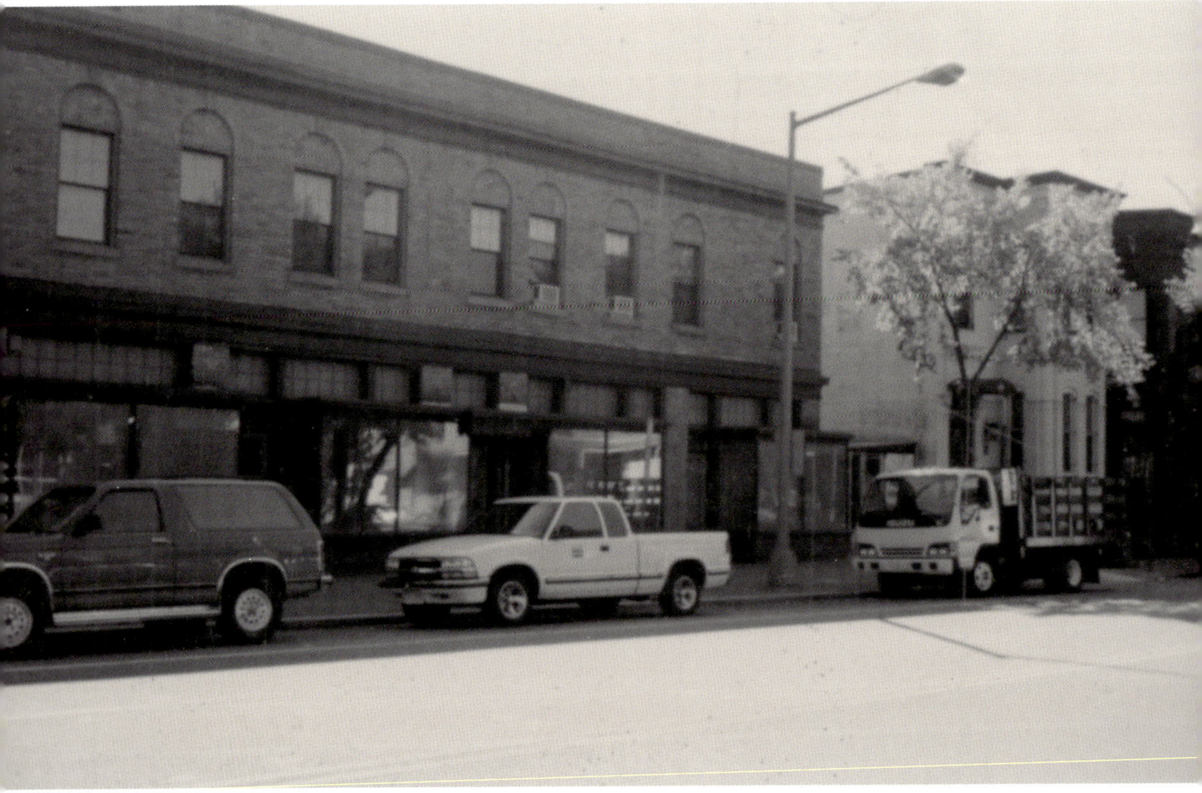

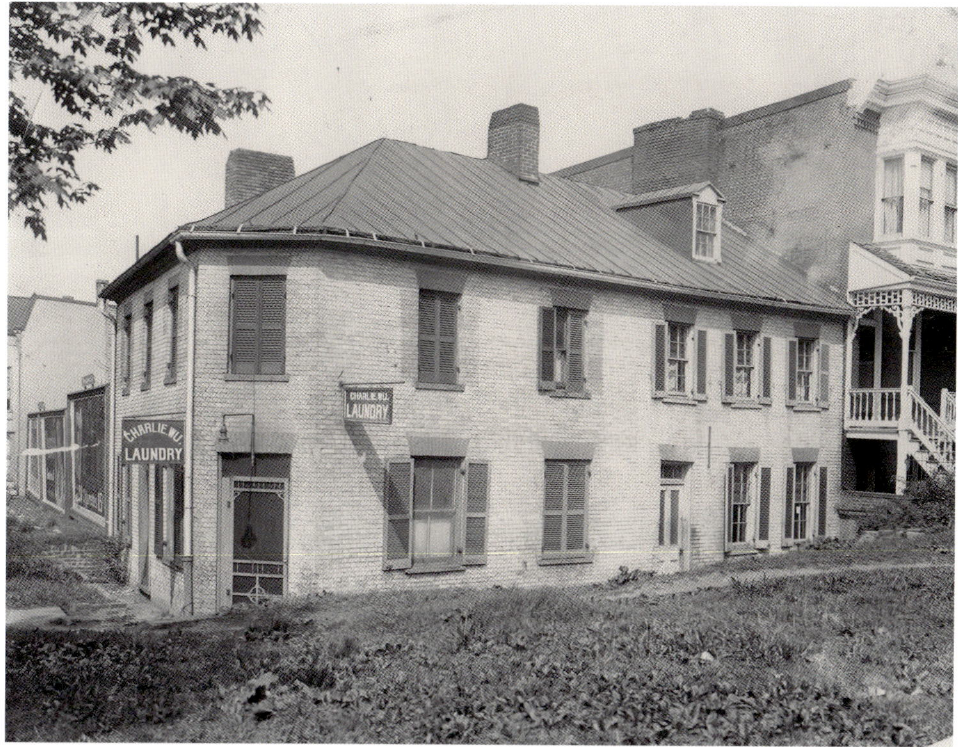

Charlie Wu, a Chinese immigrant, operated his laundry here at 461 New Jersey Avenue SE between approximately 1920 and 1928, shown in the 1920s. In 1983, Yerkes, Parker & Pappas designed an office building for S.E. Associates on the site. The past and present buildings respond to the acute angle where New Jersey Avenue meets E Street, a product of the L'Enfant Plan. (Courtesy Historical Society of Washington, DC, CHS-03454.)

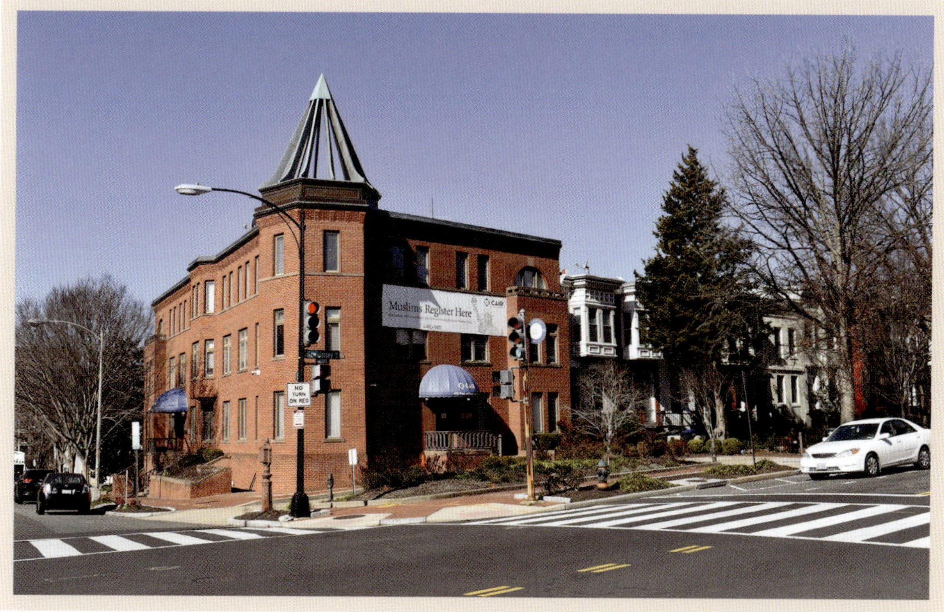

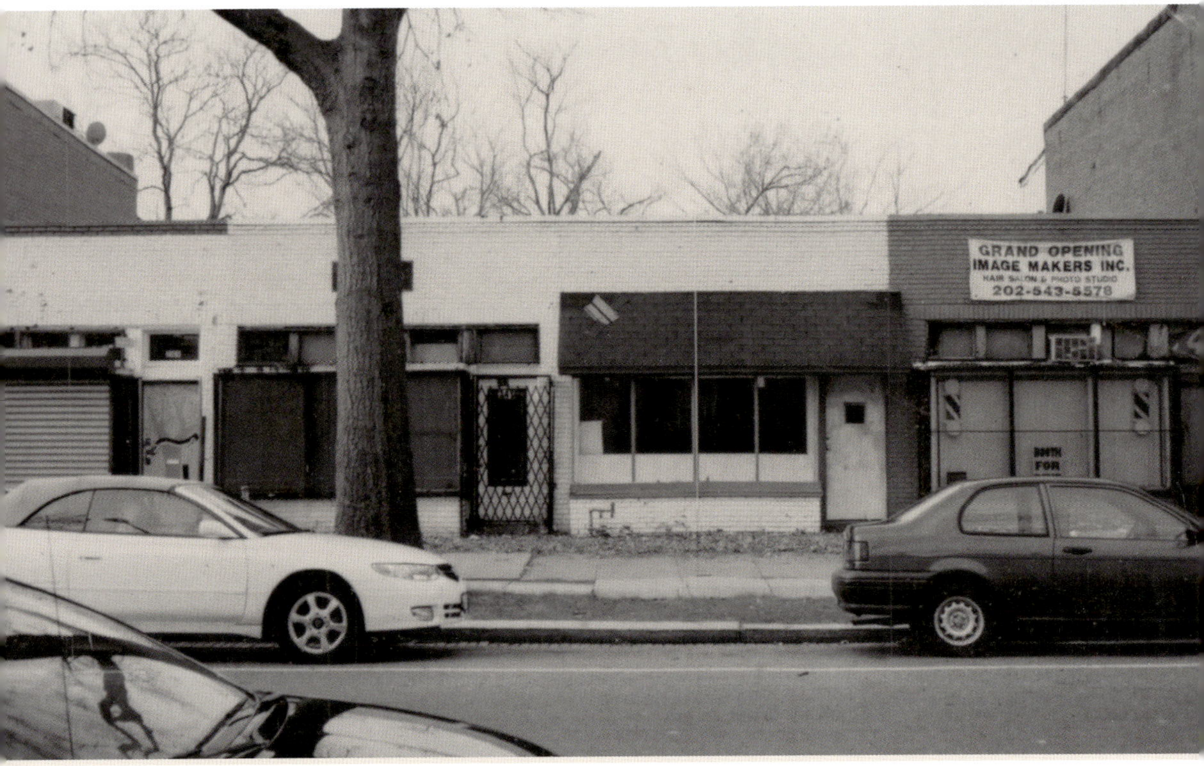

In 1924, Preston E. Wire (1903–1952), a major developer whose projects included Carver Terrace, built these one-story stores at 243–249 Fifteenth Street SE, possibly intended as "taxpayers," temporary buildings to pay carrying costs until the property could be redeveloped. Businesses, such as grocers, cleaners, variety stores, beauty salons, and later, a church, occupied the buildings until 2012, when the stores were razed and replaced by the Axis Condominium. (Author's collection.)

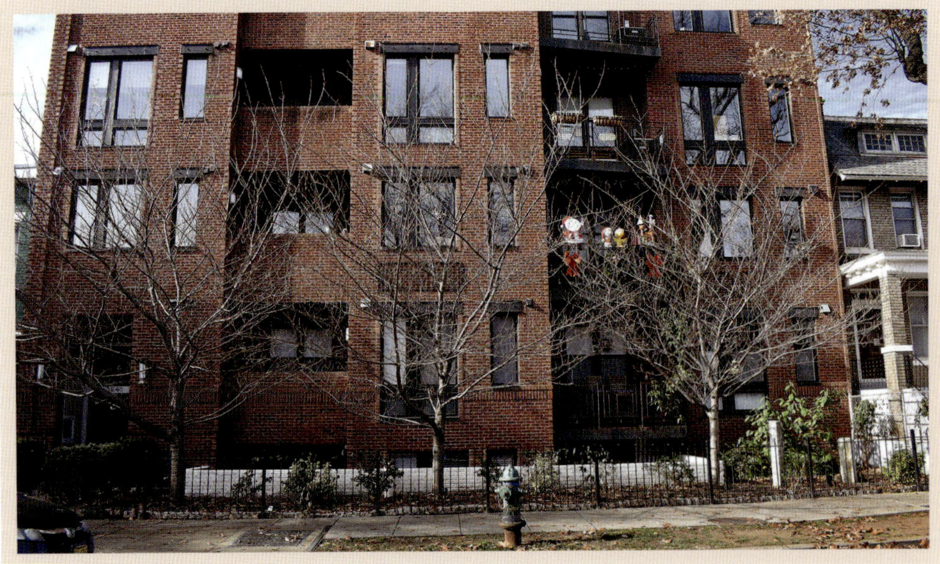

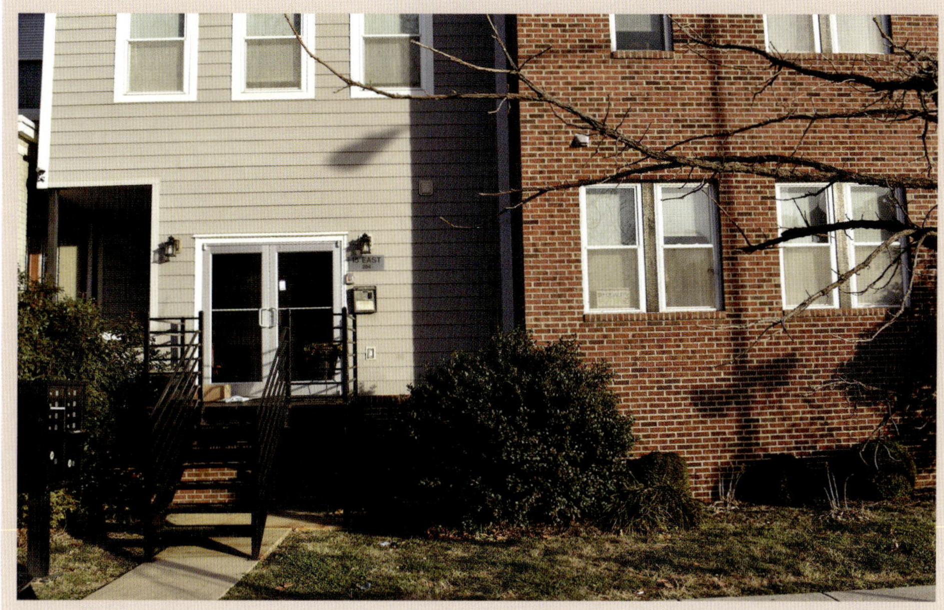

Gas stations were once found on multiple Capitol Hill corners, but many have disappeared as their sites were redeveloped. Neighbors say that this Mobilgas station at 284 Fifteenth Street SE once had a red Pegasus sign. It had closed by the late 1980s and became an informal neighborhood parking lot. Apartments were built on the site in 2010. (Author's collection.)

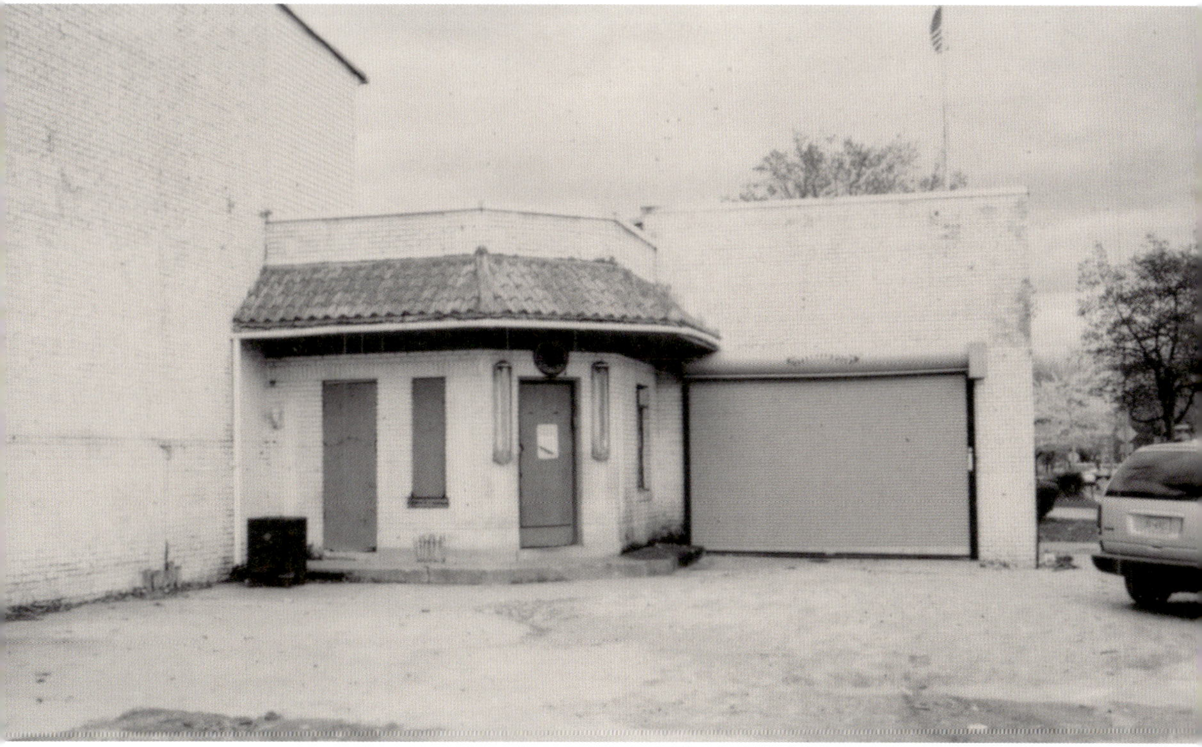

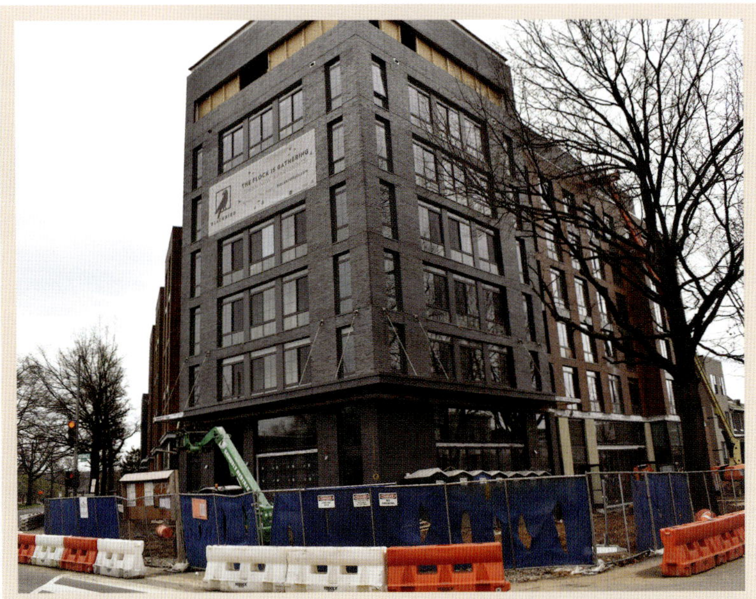

This double-pitch red roof Pizza Hut at 1401 Pennsylvania Avenue SE opened around 1986 and later became New York Pizza. The building itself formed part of Pizza Hut's corporate symbol. Drivers were attracted to the restaurant by its sign on a pylon, a practice used in Las Vegas to guide drivers moving at high speeds (perhaps not necessary on Capitol Hill). In 2020, the Blackbird, a multistory mixed-use project, replaced New York Pizza. (Author's collection.)

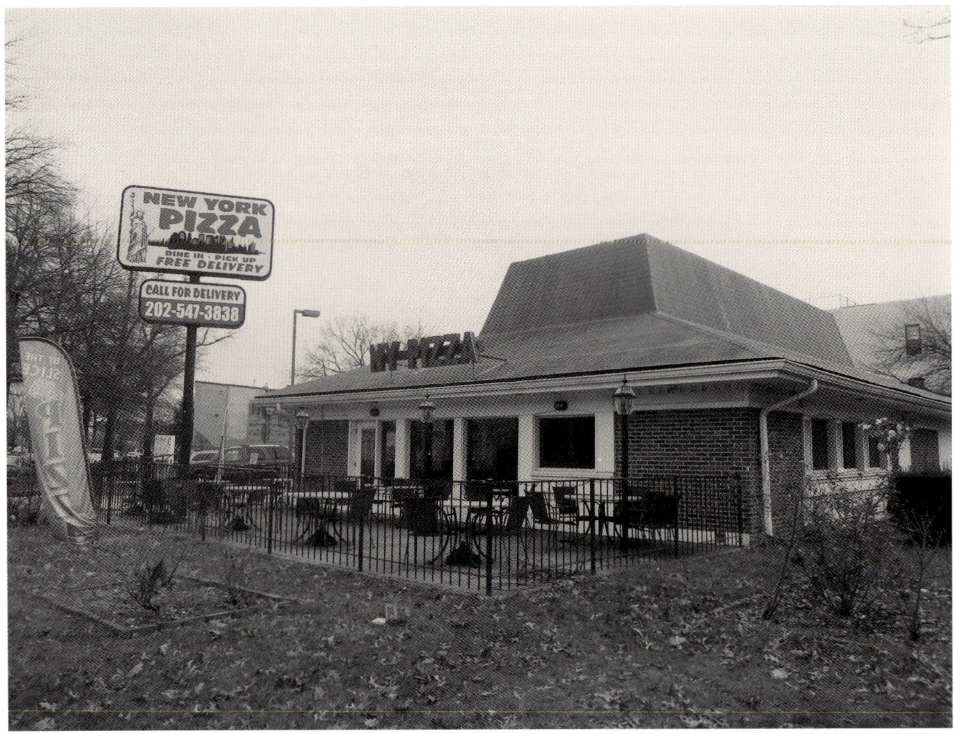

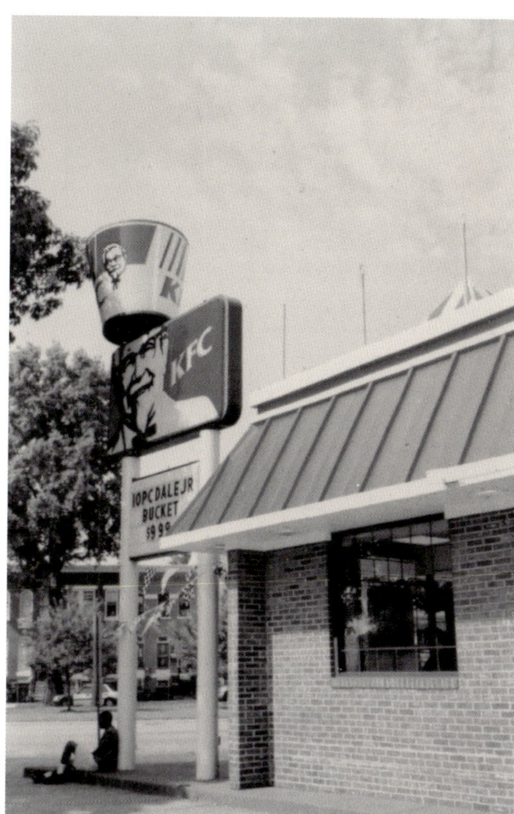

This KFC carryout at 1448 Pennsylvania Avenue SE, built in 1970, attracted customers with an oversize Colonel Sanders chicken bucket, a concept developed by Dave Thomas before he moved on to found Wendy's. In the 1990s, customers reportedly received their food through a rotating Plexiglas window. The KFC was demolished in 2007, and in 2013, Douglas Development replaced it with a two-story multiuse building. (Author's collection.)

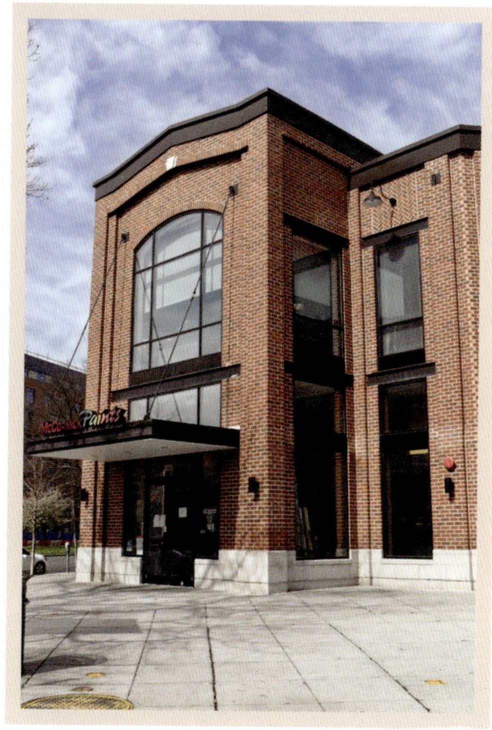

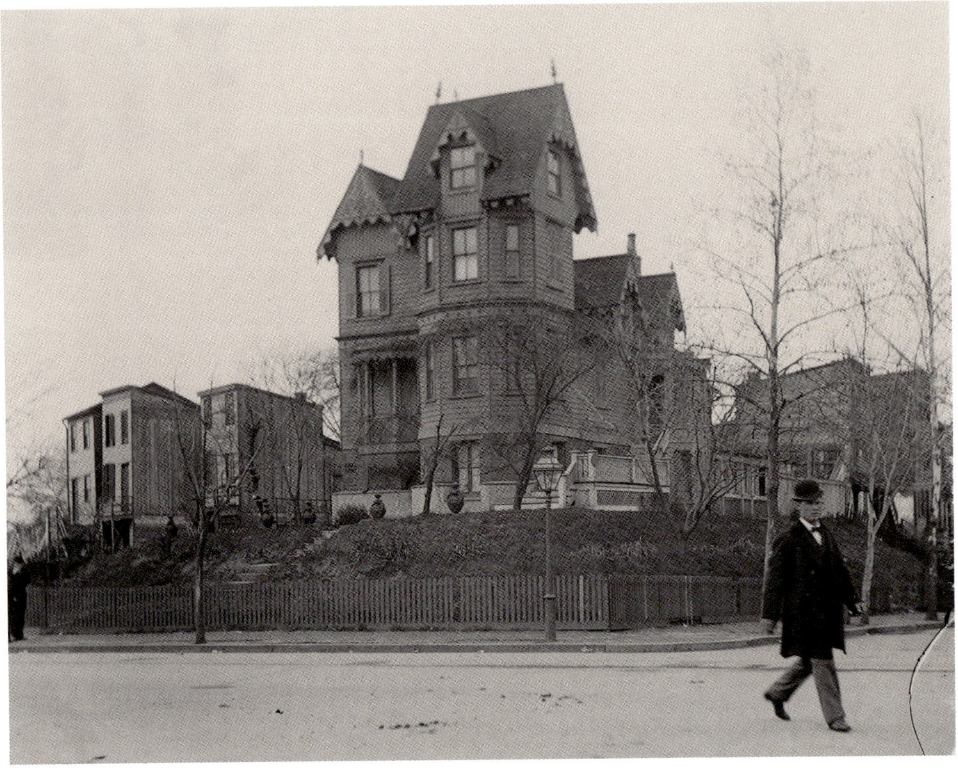

In 1873, Dr. Thomas Taylor (1820–1910), a respected chemist at the US Department of Agriculture, and his wife, Marjory, built their frame house at 238 Massachusetts Avenue NE. The polygonal tower, active roofline, crossing gables, and vergeboards combined elements from Victorian Gothic and Queen Anne. Marjory added a conservatory on the east side in 1892. The photograph dates to between 1918 and 1920. In 1926, Frank Tomlinson built a brick apartment building on the site. (Courtesy LOC, LC-F8-2546.)

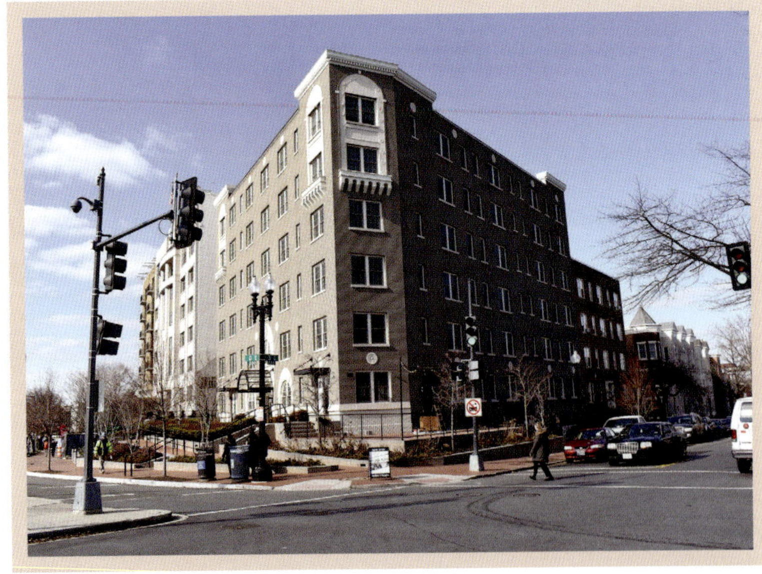

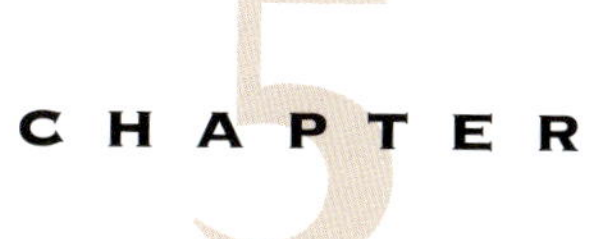

CHAPTER 5

Changes in Churches and Schools

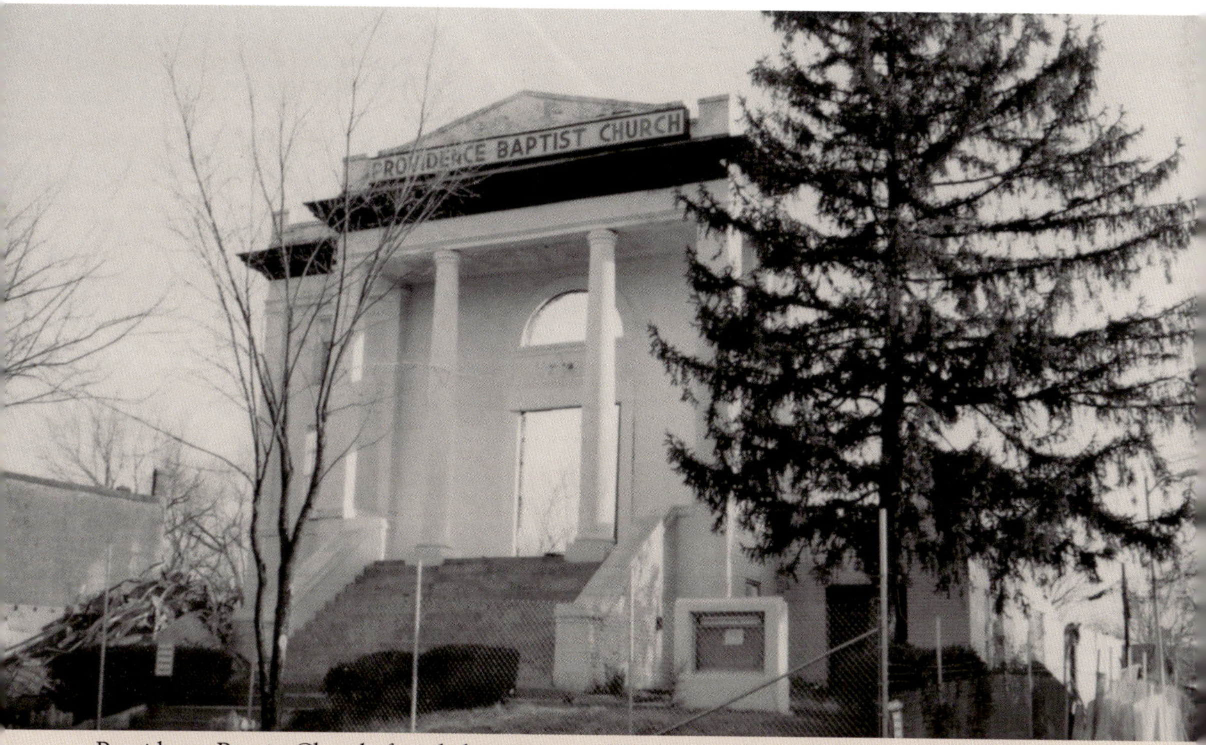

Providence Baptist Church, founded in 1891, became an African American congregation sometime before 1939 and purchased the church at 526 Fifteenth Street SE from the Fifteenth Street Christian Church in 1957, selling it in 2003. In 2005, the church was demolished and replaced by Providence Square Town Home Condominiums. The granite retaining wall is all that remains. (Author's collection.)

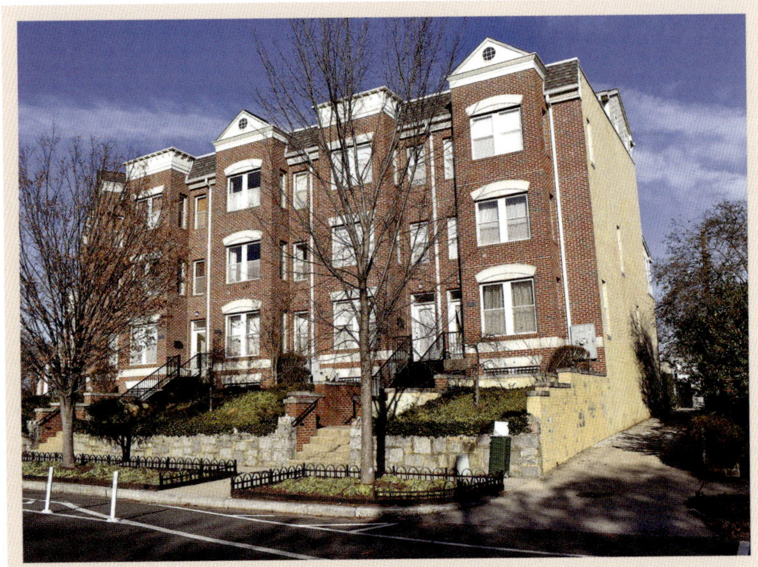

The Fifteenth Street Christian Church engaged Walter R. Metz to design an affordable Neoclassical church at 526 Fifteenth Street SE. The church was three stories and had redbrick construction with wood and stone trim. Two massive columns supported the porch. The central doors had four lights each with a transom above and a fan light over the door. Condominiums now occupy the site. (Photograph by John P. Wymer; courtesy Historical Society of Washington, DC, WY-1450.)

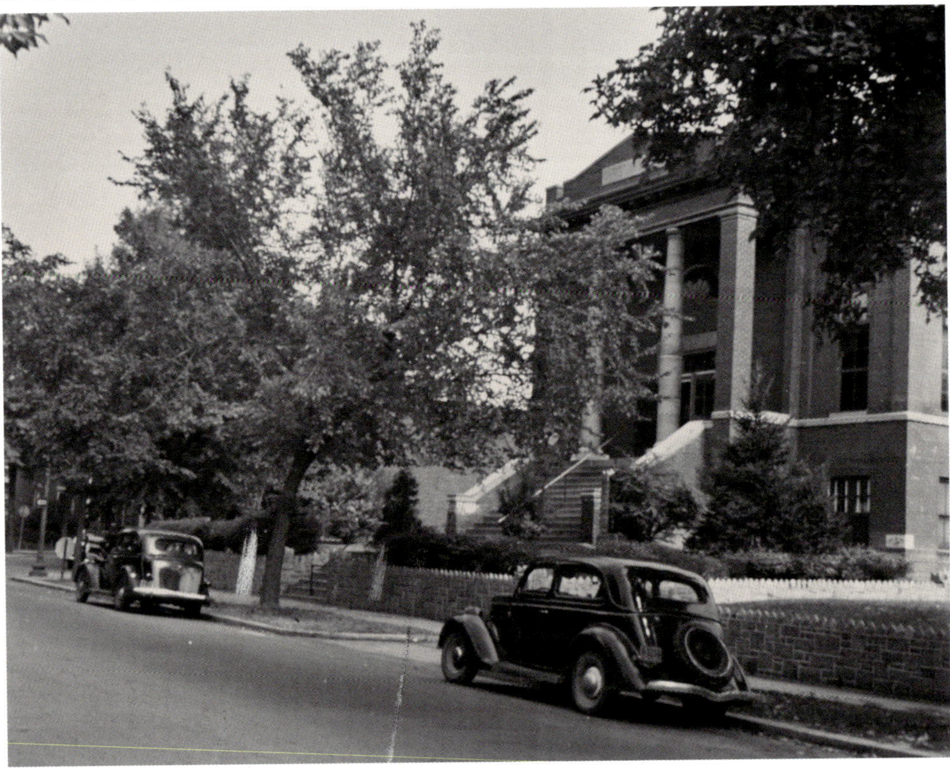

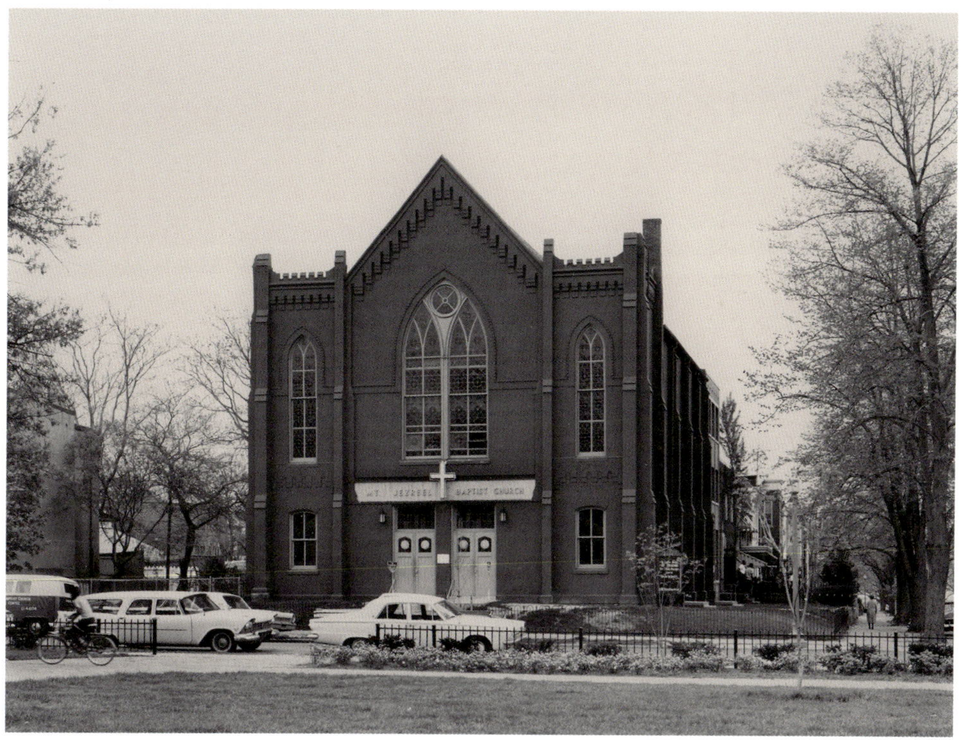

In 1884, formerly enslaved people built Mount Jezreel Baptist Church at 501 E Street SE, designed by the African American architect Calvin T.S. Brent. In the 1980s, members debated razing the church and building a new one. The congregation decided to move. The church remains, now the home of Progress for Christ Baptist Church. It is shown in 1965, before formstone (a three-layer stucco product) was applied. (Photograph by William E. Barrett; courtesy Historical Society of Washington, DC, KC-2144.)

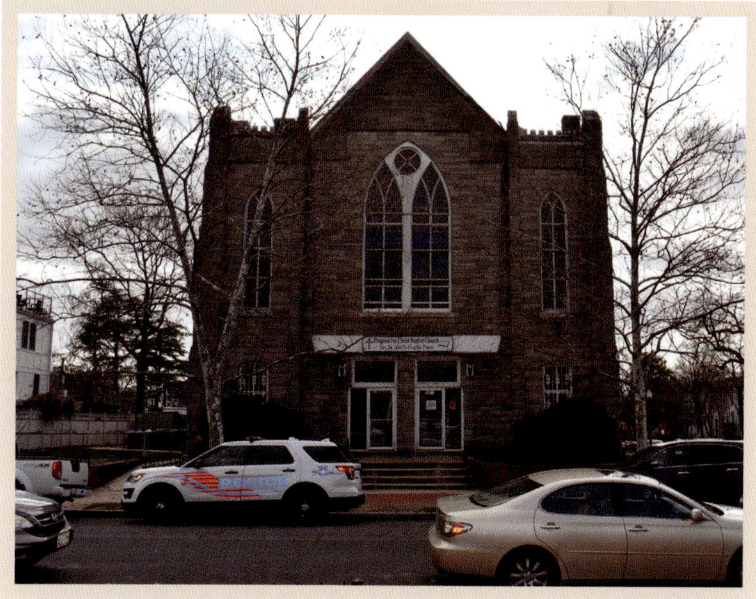

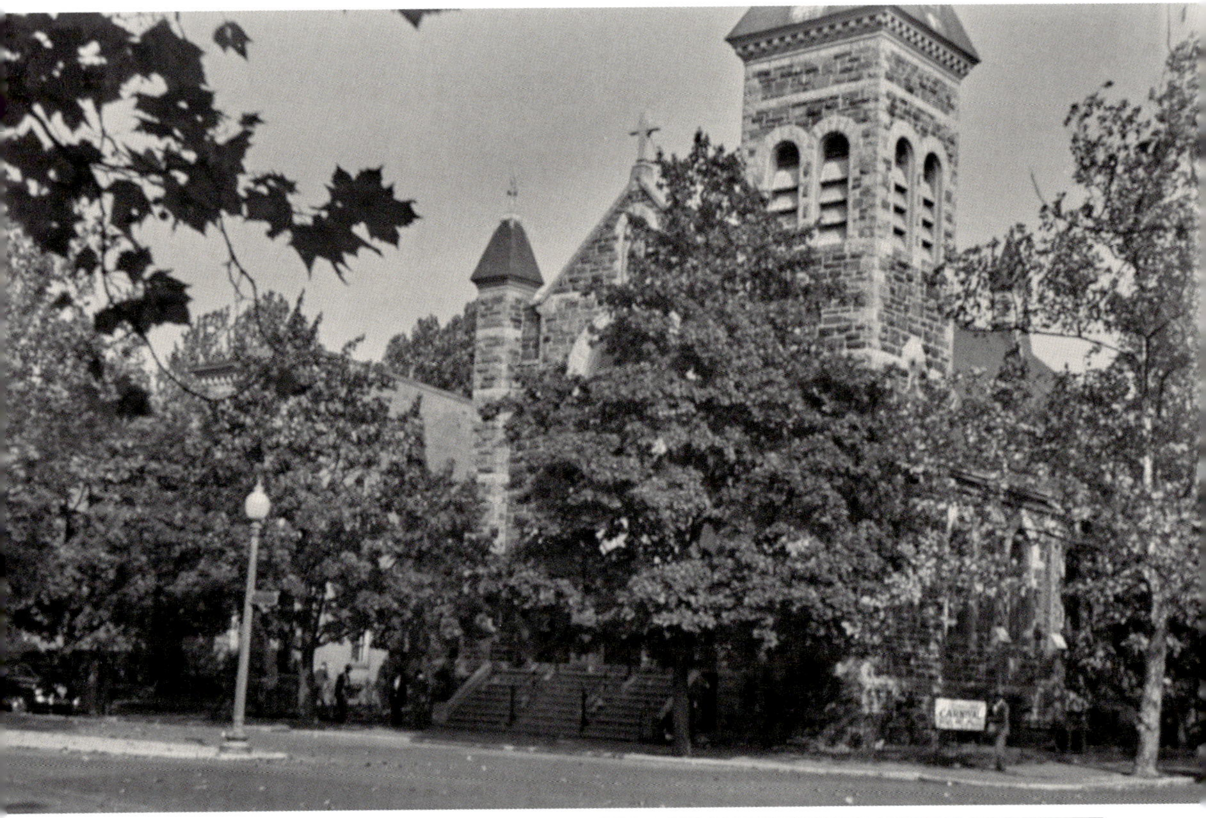

A plaque at Thirteenth and C Streets SE reads "The parish of St Cyprian was established in 1893 by . . . Black Catholics. . . . Through the financial sacrifices and physical labor of the parishioners St. Cyprian church was built [at 1238 C Street SE]. This parish . . . joined the parish of Holy Comforter to form the church of Holy Comforter – St. Cyprian in 1966." In 1972, row houses were built here. (Photograph by John P. Wymer; courtesy Historical Society of Washington, DC, WY-1455.)

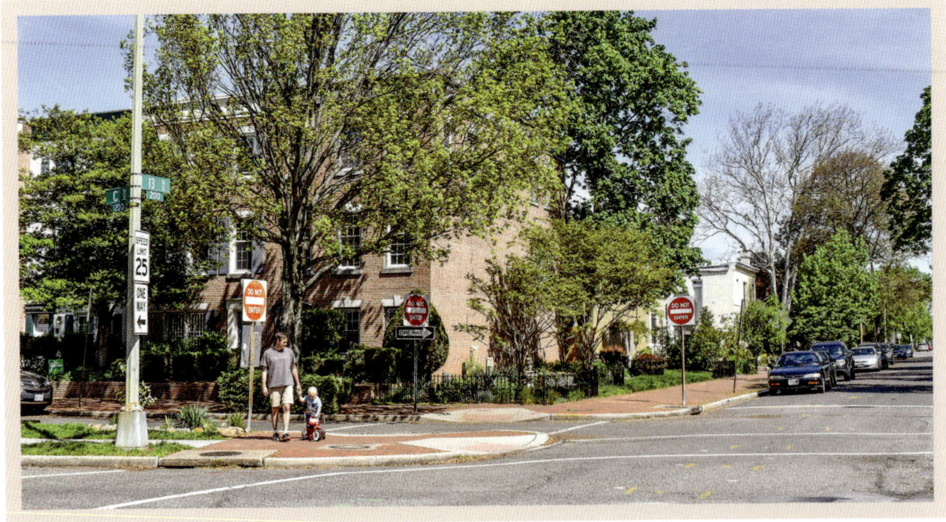

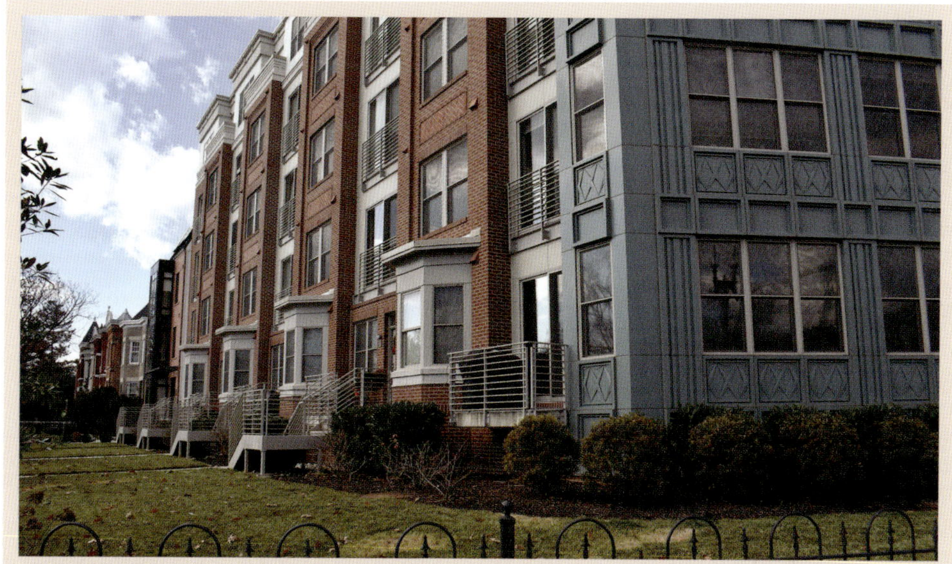

The Maryland Avenue Baptist Church, at 1354 Maryland Avenue NE, was built in 1928 and appears in this 1950 photograph. Refreshing Springs Church of God in Christ bought the church building in 1964. The church was demolished to construct the Maryland condominiums in 2015. (Photograph by John P. Wymer; courtesy Historical Society of Washington, DC, WY1265.)

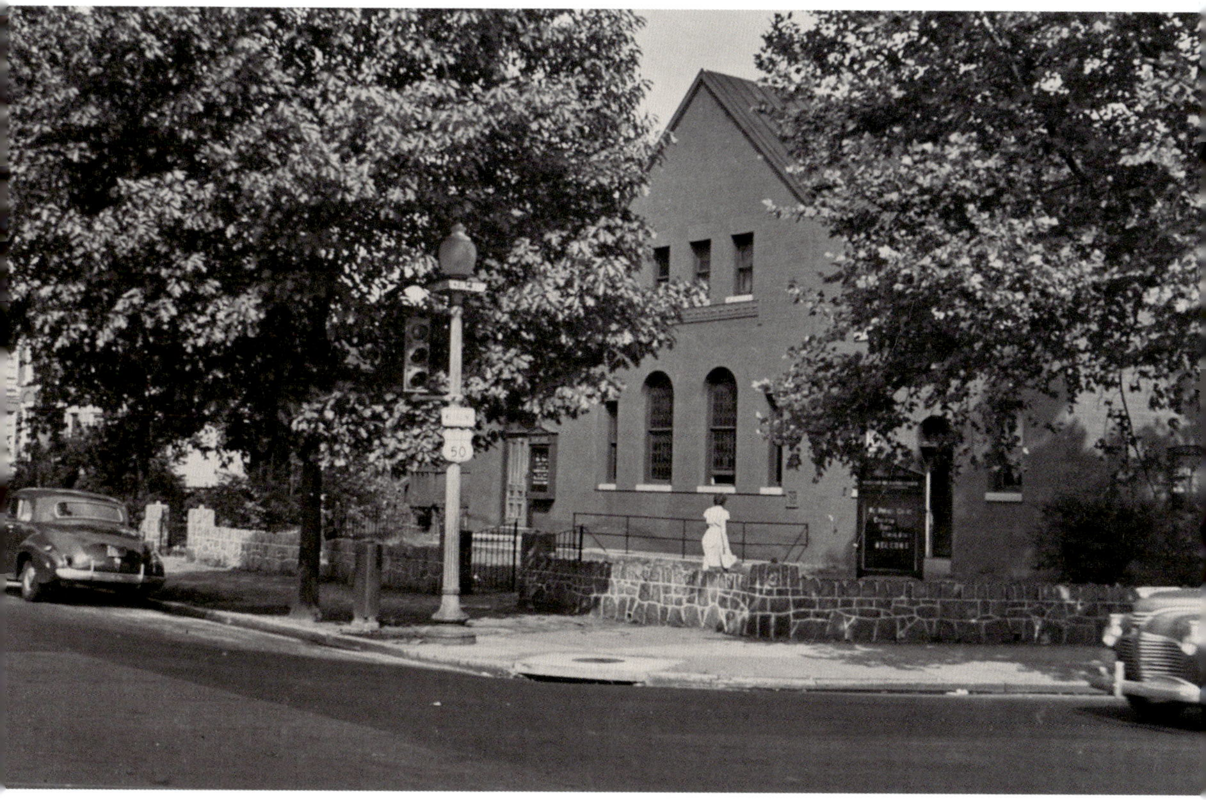

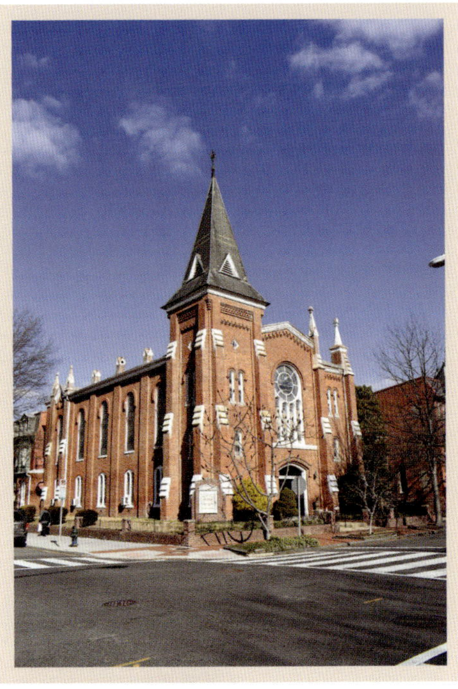

Waugh Methodist Episcopal Church, an integrated congregation, built their church at 300 A Street NE in 1858. It has American bond brick coursing. The stained-glass windows feature anthemions, a design from ancient Egypt. It is pictured between 1910 and 1919, when it was painted white. The paint was removed by 1965. Today, Faith Tabernacle United Holy Church of America uses the building. (Photograph by Willard R. Ross; courtesy Historical Society of Washington, DC, CHS-08733.)

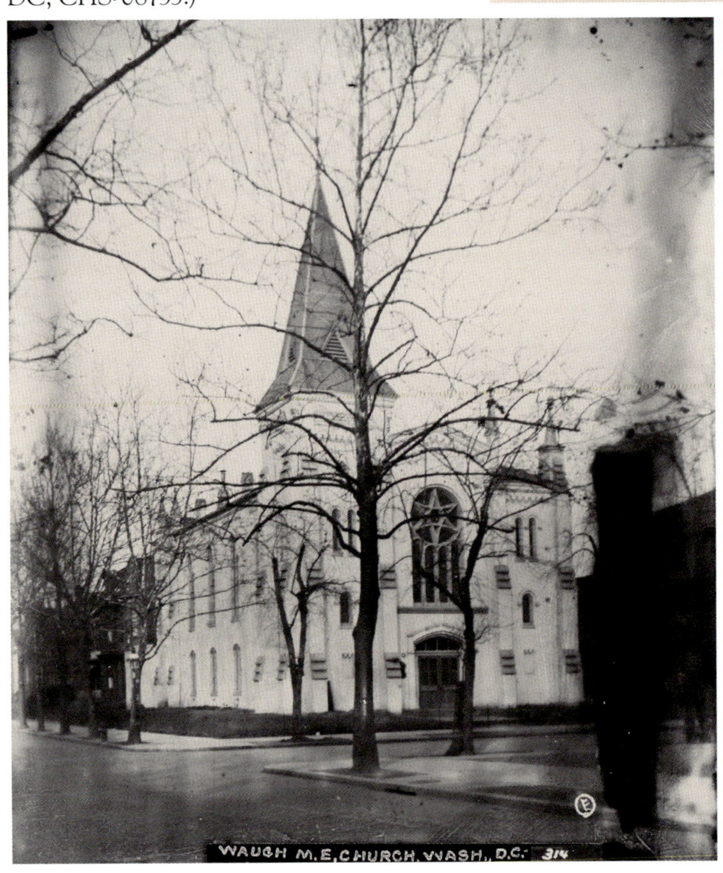

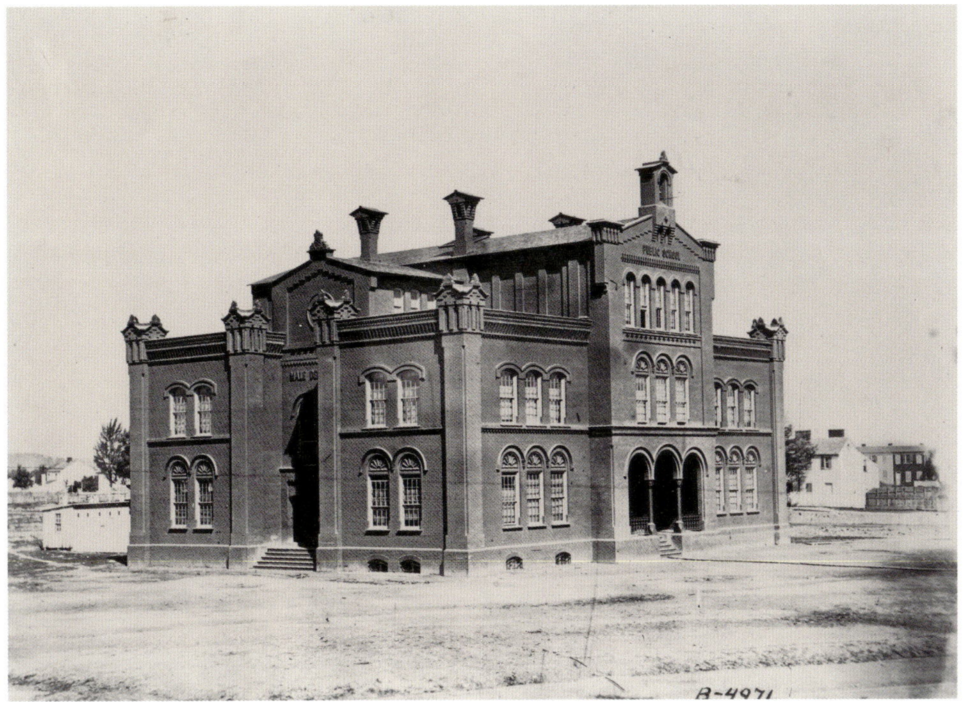

In 1866, Adolph Cluss designed Wallach School, facing Pennsylvania Avenue SE. It was the first public school in Square 901 (Seventh/Eighth/C/D Streets SE), a square dedicated to public schools from 1866 to 2007. Wallach School was demolished in 1949 to construct the new Hine Junior High School for white students, which was replaced in 2015 by office/retail/residential development. (Courtesy Historical Society of Washington, DC, BI-048.)

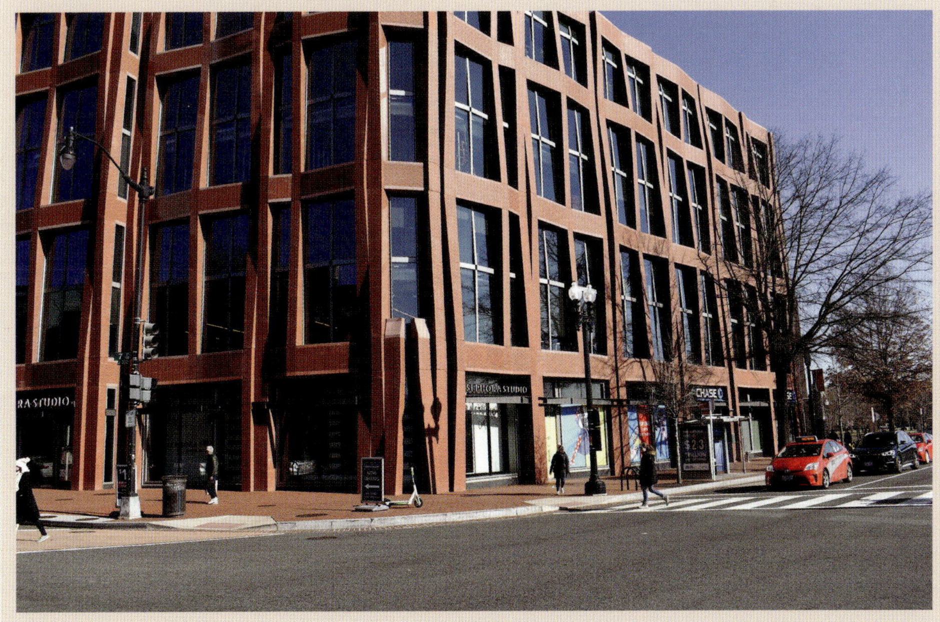

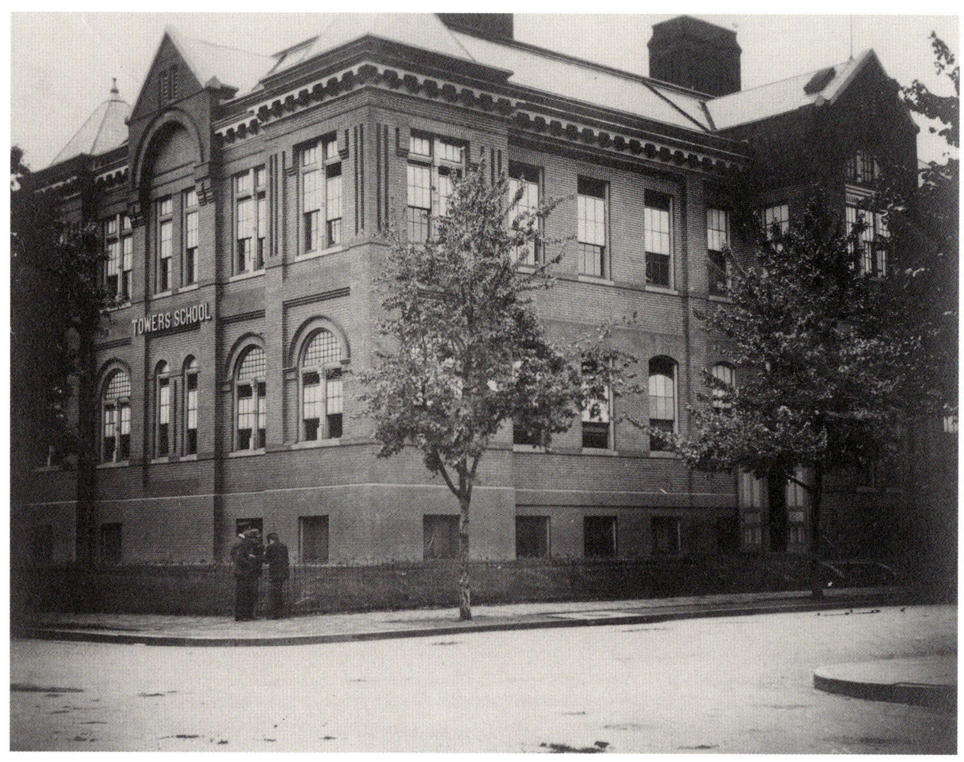

In 1887, Towers School, named for Mayor John T. Towers (1811–1857), was built for white students at Eighth and C Streets SE in Square 901 and demolished between 1949 and 1956. As of 2018, as part of the redevelopment of Square 901, the apartment building at 333 Eighth Street SE occupies the site. (Courtesy Historical Society of Washington, DC, PSC-120.)

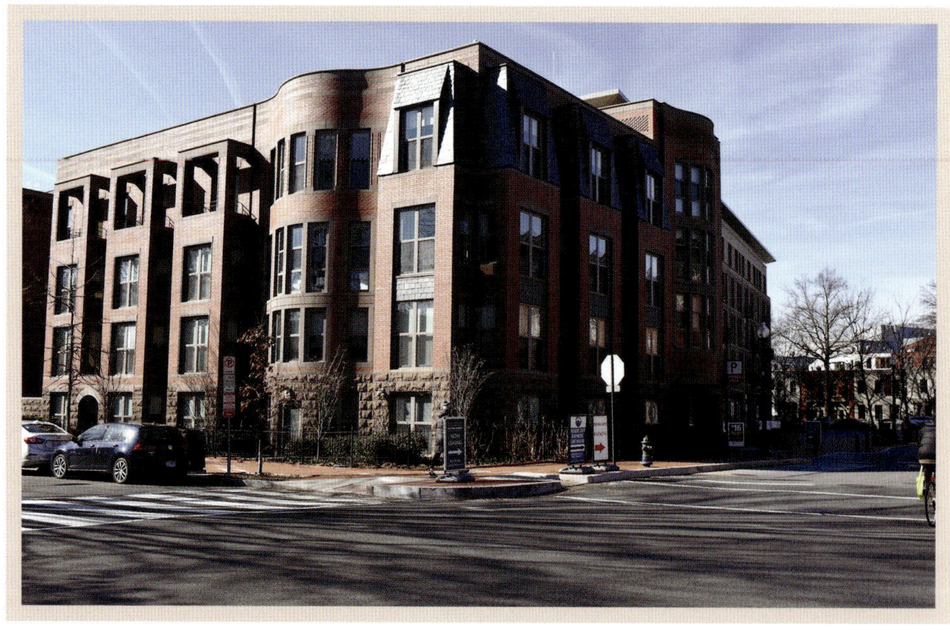

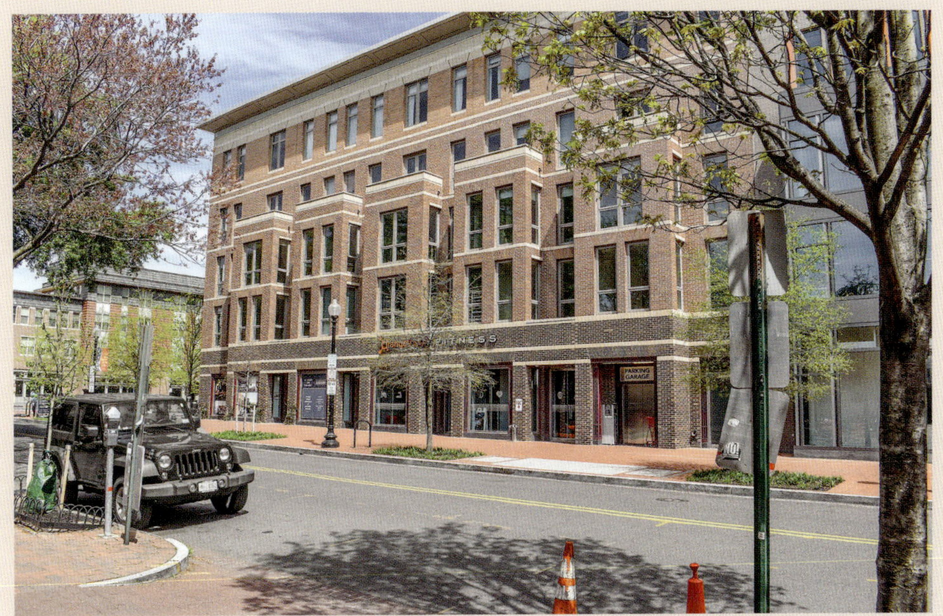

Eastern High School, built in 1892 on the 300 block of Seventh Street SE in Square 901, was converted to a junior high school in 1923 after a new high school opened on East Capitol Street NE. This school was sometimes referred to as "old" Hine Junior High School and was demolished around 1967. The site, 330 Seventh Street SE, is now office/retail/residential development. (Photograph by William E. Barrett; courtesy Historical of Washington, DC, KC-3045-PHWBLU.)

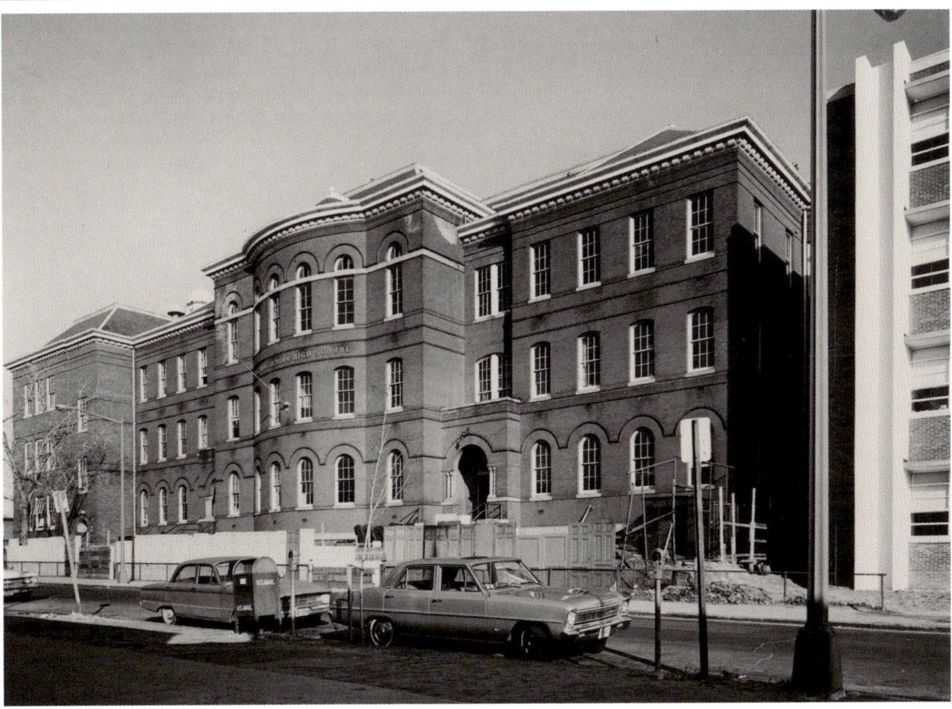

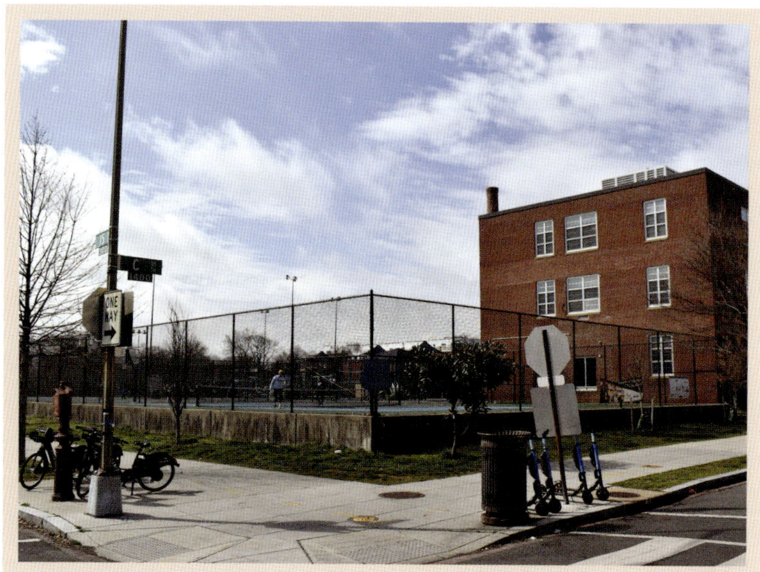

In 1896, the Board of Education authorized building Payne Elementary School for African American students. A typical eight-room schoolhouse at the corner of Fifteenth and C Streets SE, it served students until approximately 1980. In 1983, a fire severely damaged the vacant building, and the board decided to raze the school and replace it with tennis courts. Payne's 1953 wing is visible in the present photograph. (Courtesy Charles Sumner School Museum and Archives.)

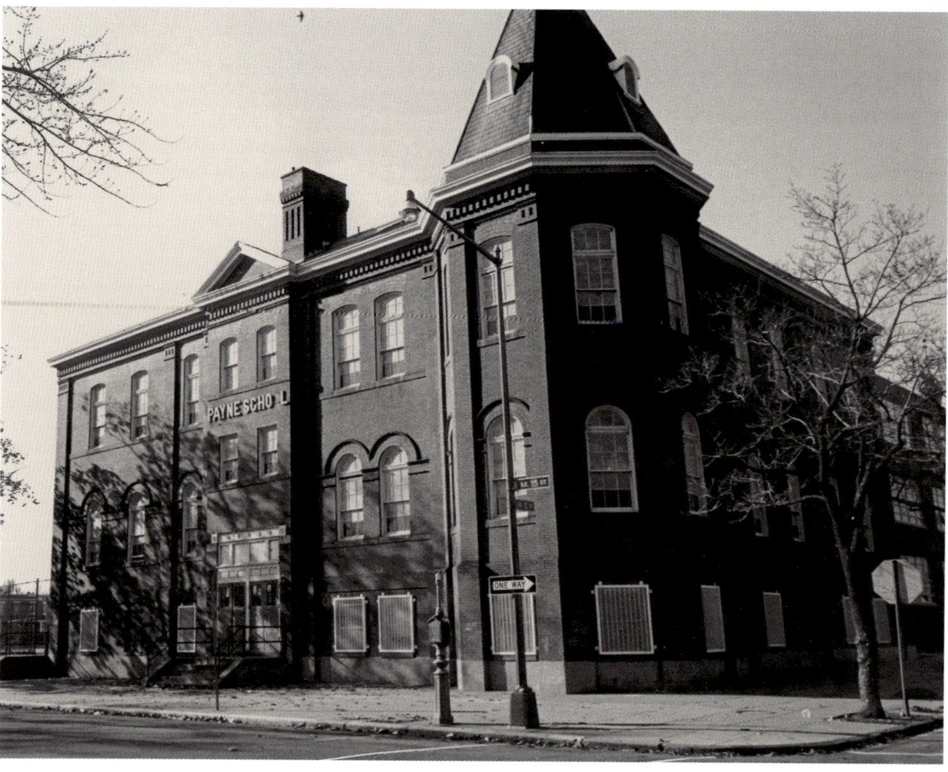

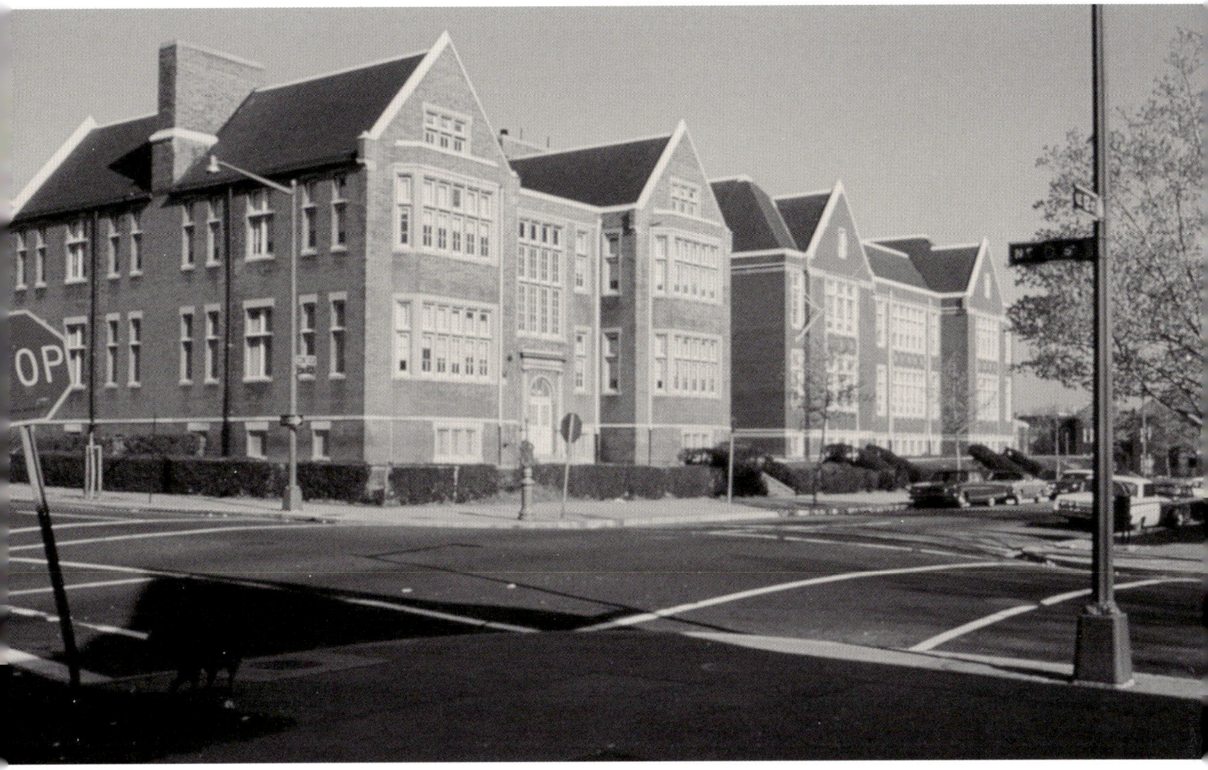

Lovejoy School is named for abolitionist Elijah P. Lovejoy. Its three buildings at Twelfth and D Streets NE were built in stages, from left to right, 1901 (light-brown brick), 1922 (redbrick), and 2004 (brown brick, by Winter Properties) in one design—a split-gable roof with shallow two-story bays. DC Public Schools sold the school around 2003, and it is now Lovejoy Lofts. (Photograph by Emil A. Press; courtesy Historical Society of Washington, DC, PR-1672A.)

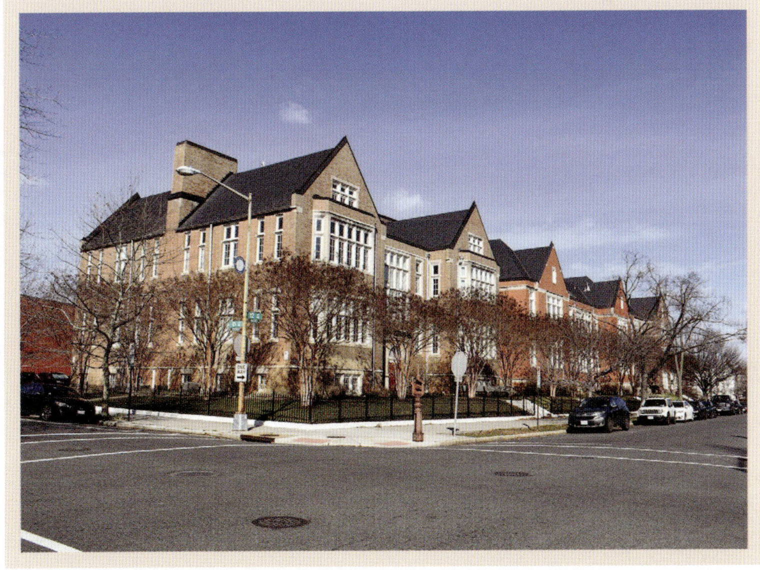

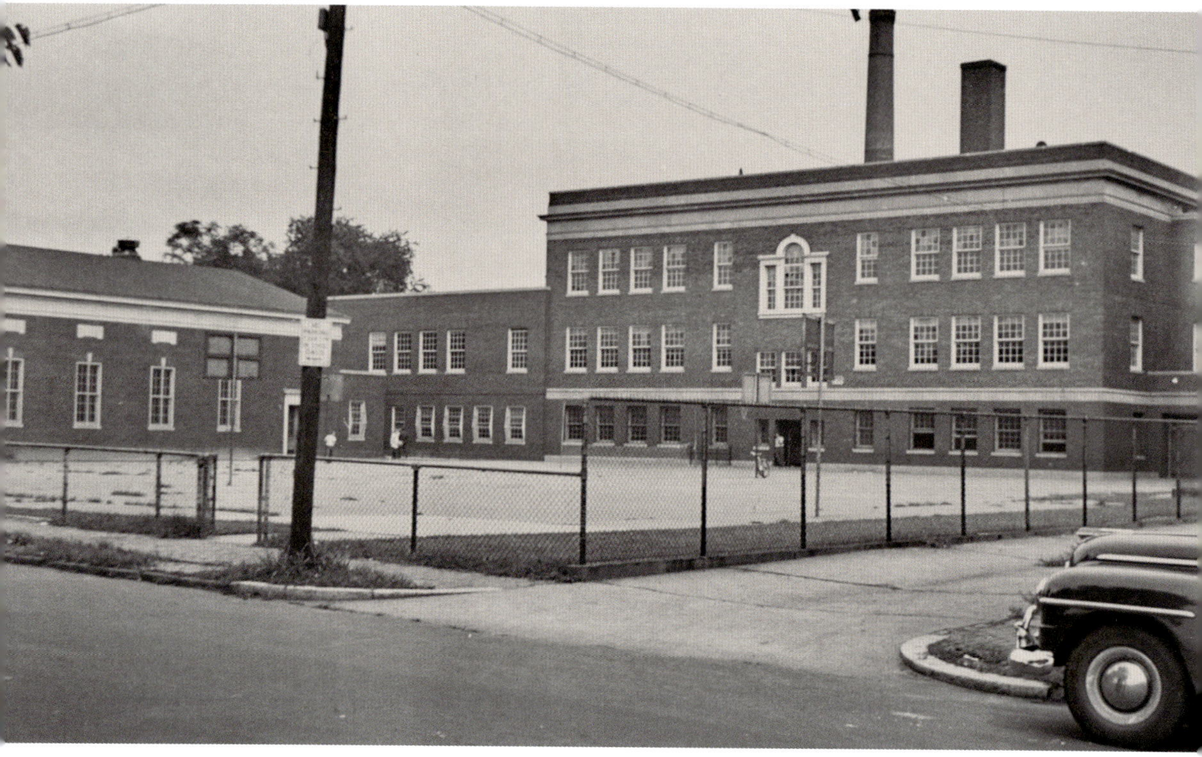

The Buchanan School complex on the 1300 blocks of D and E Streets SE was built in 1895, 1921, 1930, and around 1960. The 1895 Romanesque Revival building facing E Street SE and the 1921 building to its north remain. The 1930 and the c. 1960 buildings on D Street were razed in 2017 to construct 32 row houses at Thirteenth and D Streets. (Photograph by John P. Wymer; courtesy Historical Society of Washington, DC, WY-1469.)

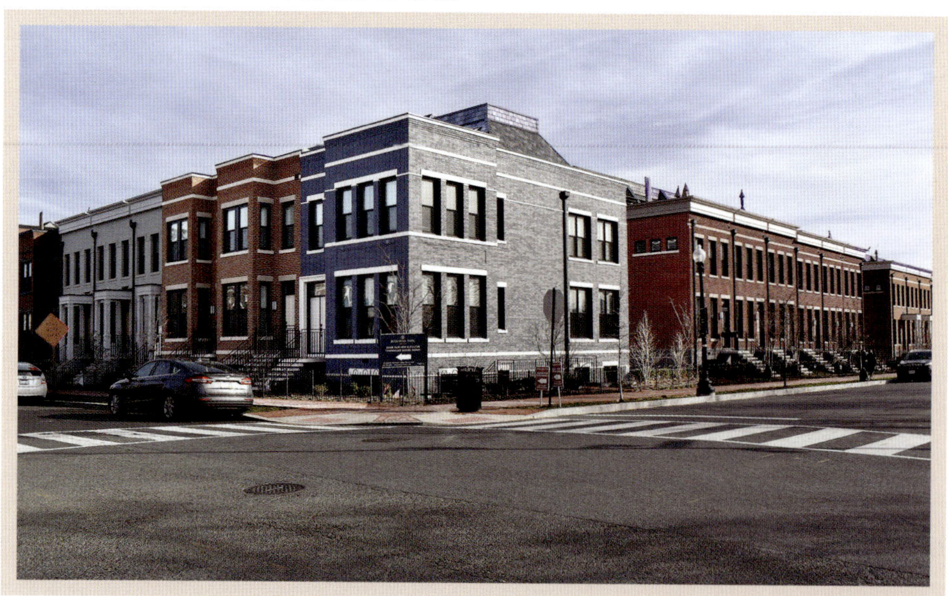

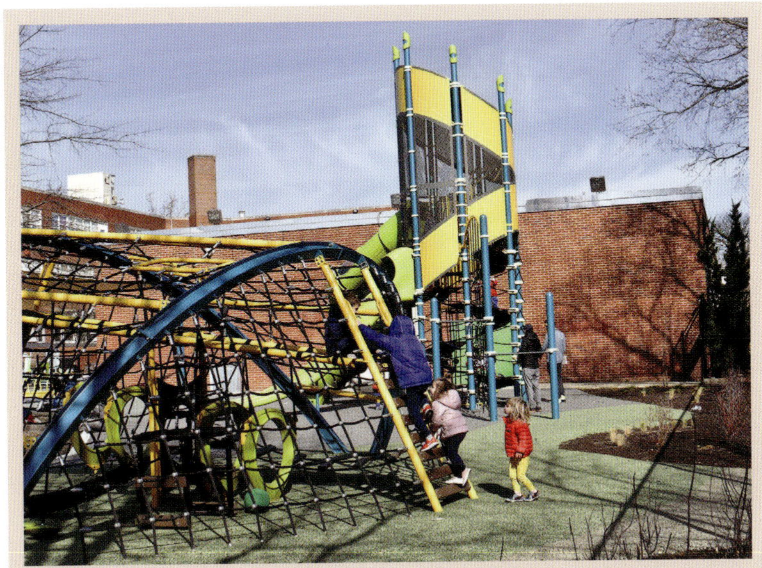

The original Tyler School, built in 1890 for African American students and named for Pres. John Tyler, was a typical eight-room schoolhouse. Located on the west side of Eleventh Street between G and I Streets SE, it is shown between 1895 and 1905. After a new school was built in 1949, the original building was razed to become part of the school playground. (Courtesy Historical Society of Washington, DC, PSC-122.)

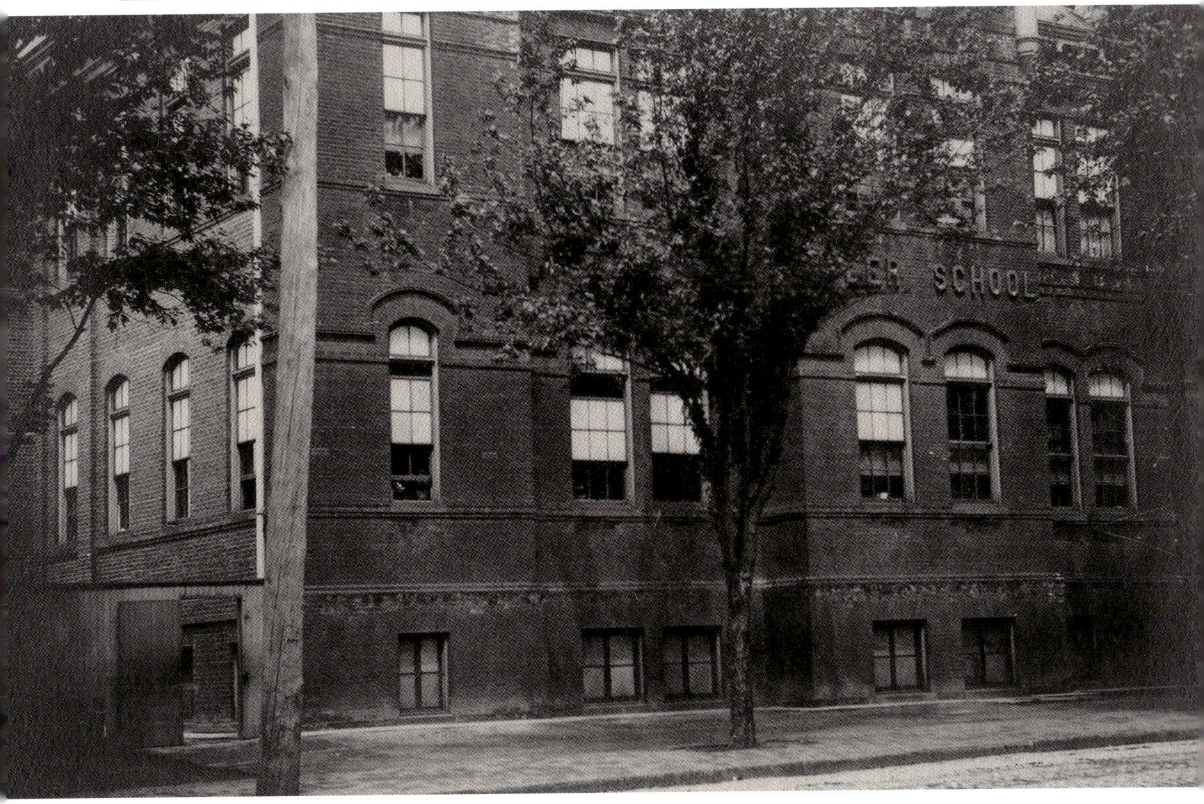

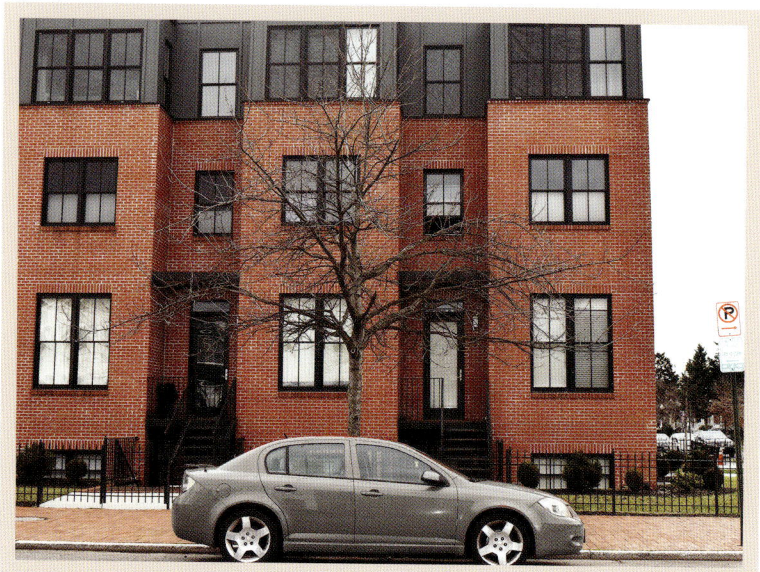

Cranch School, Twelfth and G Streets SE, was named for William Cranch (1769–1855), chief judge of the US Circuit Court of the District of Columbia. Built in 1872, the school added a third story in 1903. Cranch, Wallach, and the original Tyler School were demolished and replaced by a new Tyler School. The Cranch site was occupied next by a Salvation Army building and then by Cambridge Row in 2014. (Photograph by Alexander Gardner; courtesy Charles Sumner School Museum and Archives.)

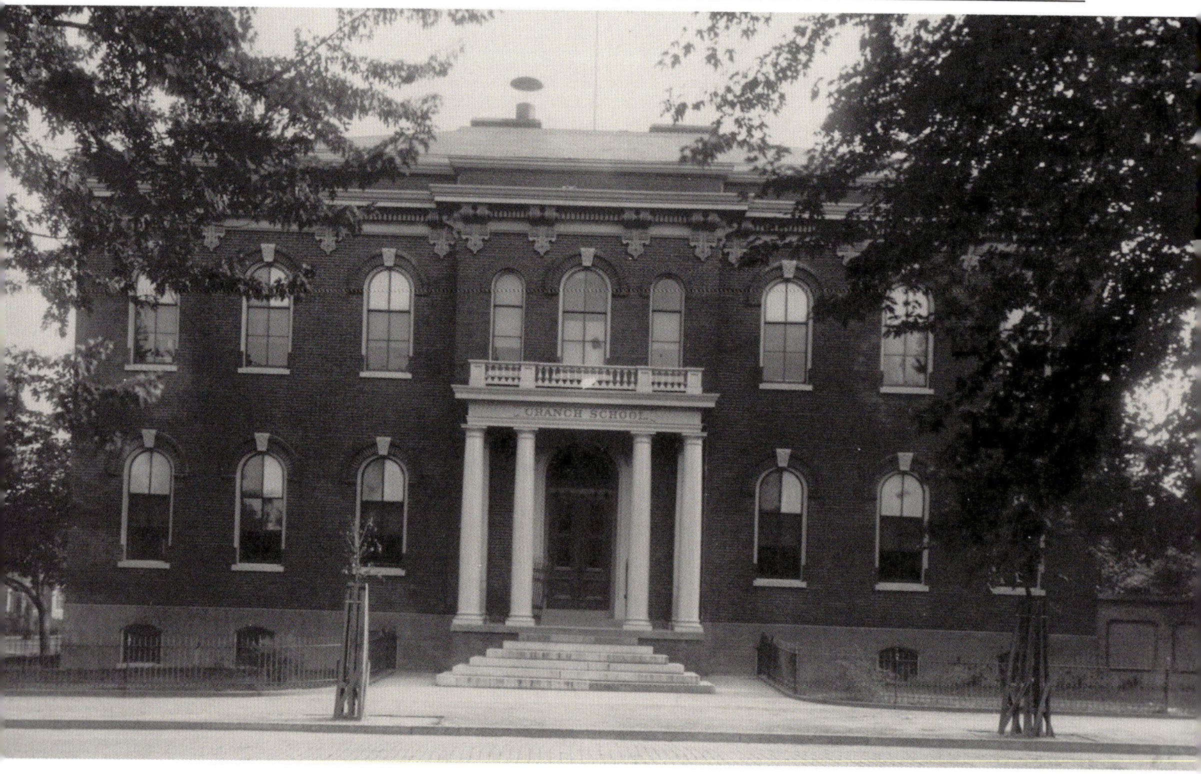

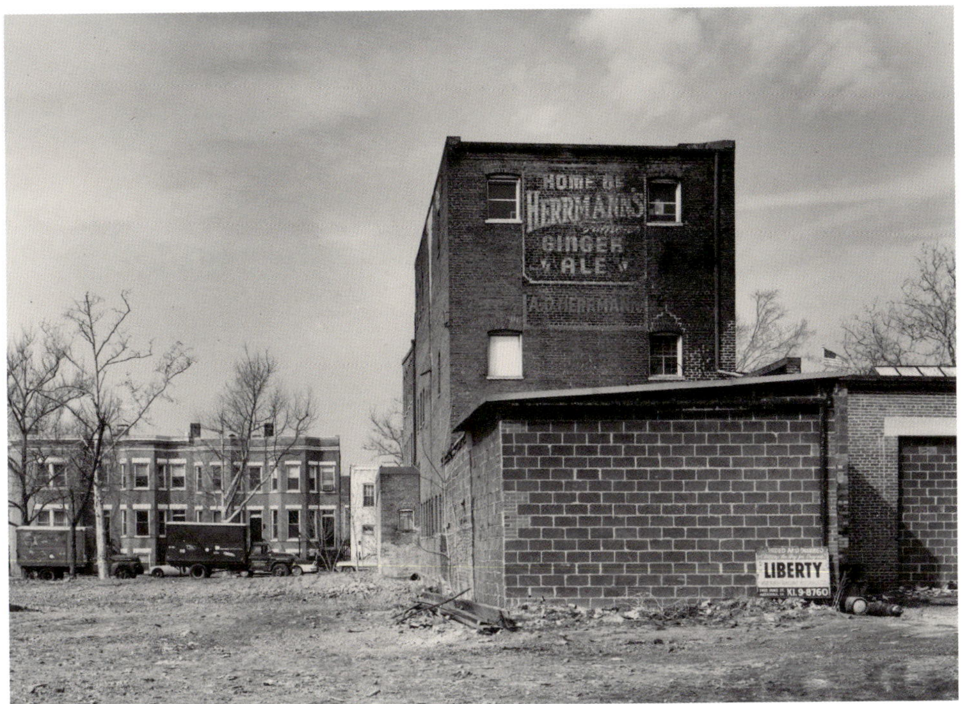

Hermann Bottling Works, a brewery, opened in 1874, moved to 750 Tenth Street SE in 1885, and was renamed the Hermann Ginger Ale Company in 1932. The name is visible on the rear wall at 750 Tenth Street in this 1967 photograph. The row houses at 773–767 Tenth Street SE (from left to right) remain. Hermann's was one of 30 buildings razed for the playing field at Tyler School. (Photograph by William E. Barrett; courtesy Historical of Washington, KC-2125.)

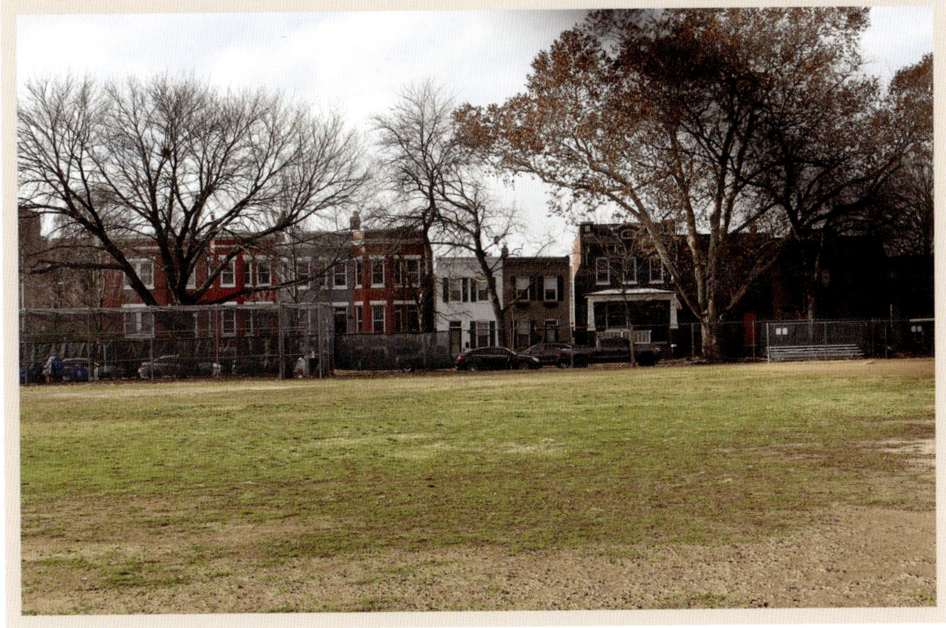

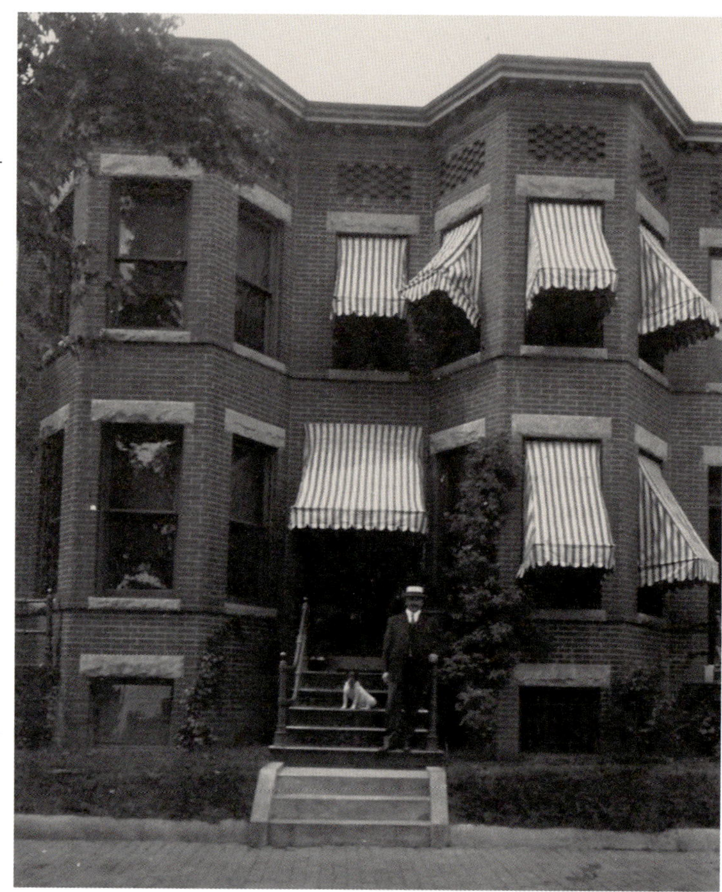

Hans Wunderlich (1865–1923), a German immigrant, appears with his dog Archie at his house at 718 C Street SE in 1920. He played the cornet in the US Marine Band. His widow, Emilie, lived here until her death in 1958. In 1964, C Street was closed, and these row houses were demolished for the Hine Junior High School playground. In 2017, C Street was reopened, and senior citizens' affordable housing was built here. (Courtesy Nancy Metzger.)

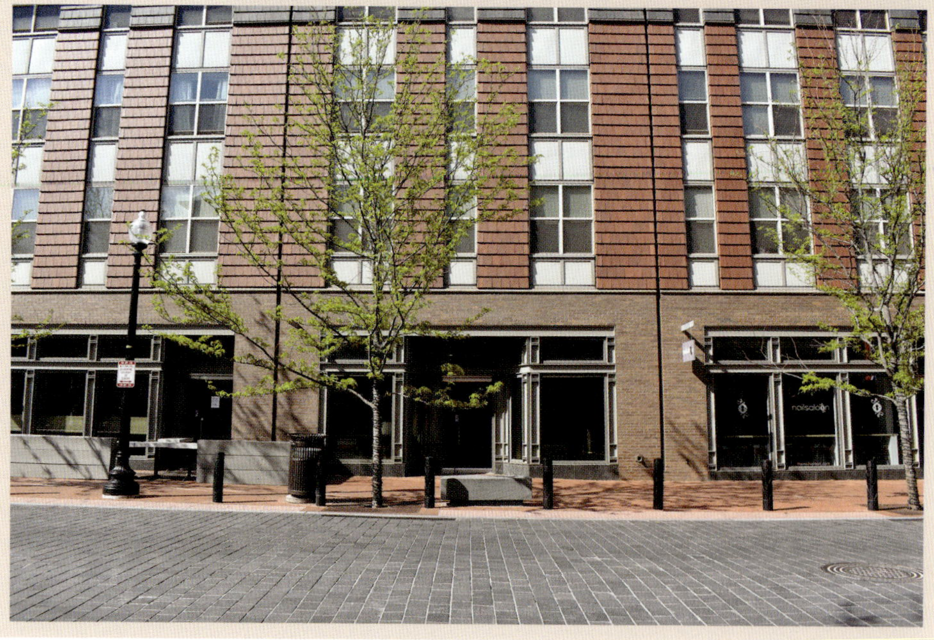

CHAPTER 6

Disappearing Alley Dwellings

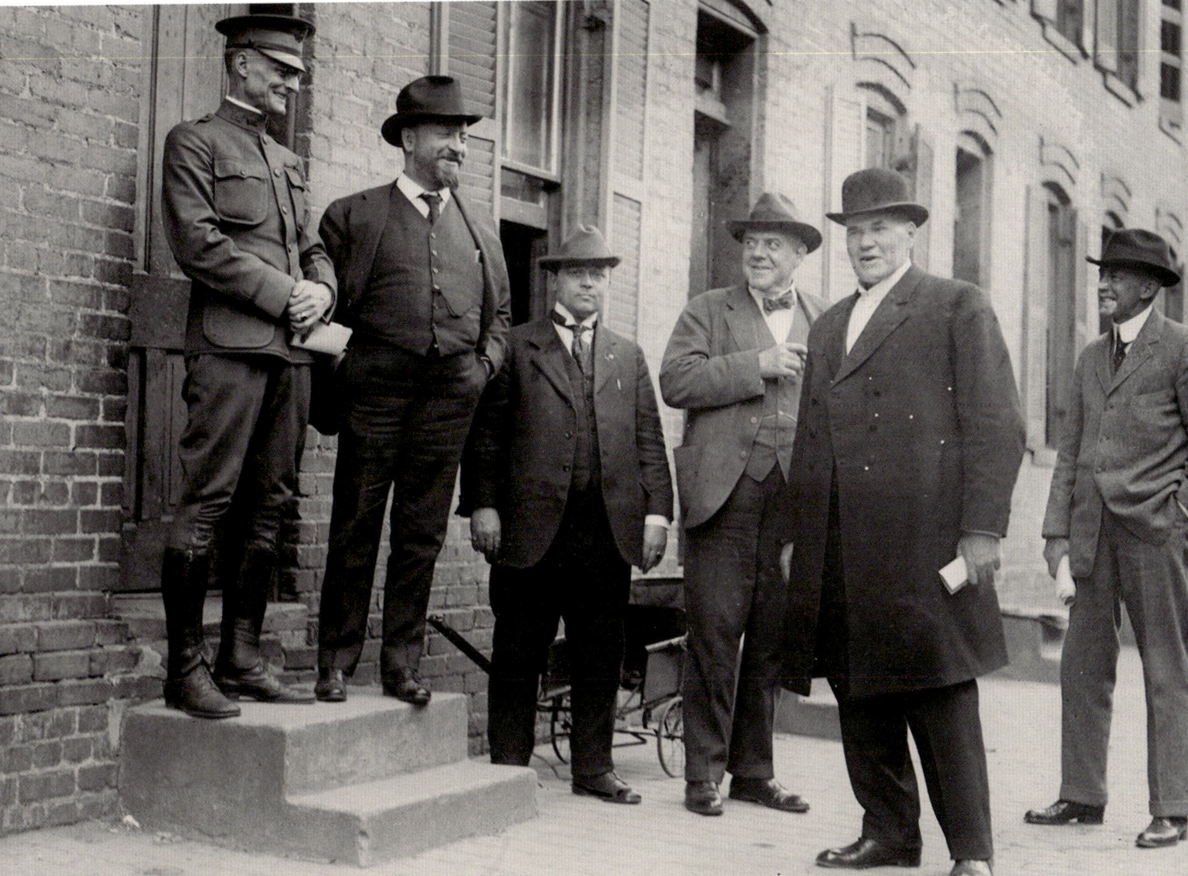

There were 70 dwellings and four stores in Navy Place SE (Sixth/Seventh/G/I Streets SE in Square 878), described as "picturesquely squalid" in a 1930 news article. This photograph shows a special House of Representatives committee inspecting the alley in 1920. From left to right are unidentified, Representative Tinckham, Rev. J. Milton Waldron (?), Commissioner Katz (?), and two unidentified. (Courtesy LOC, LC-F8-7832.)

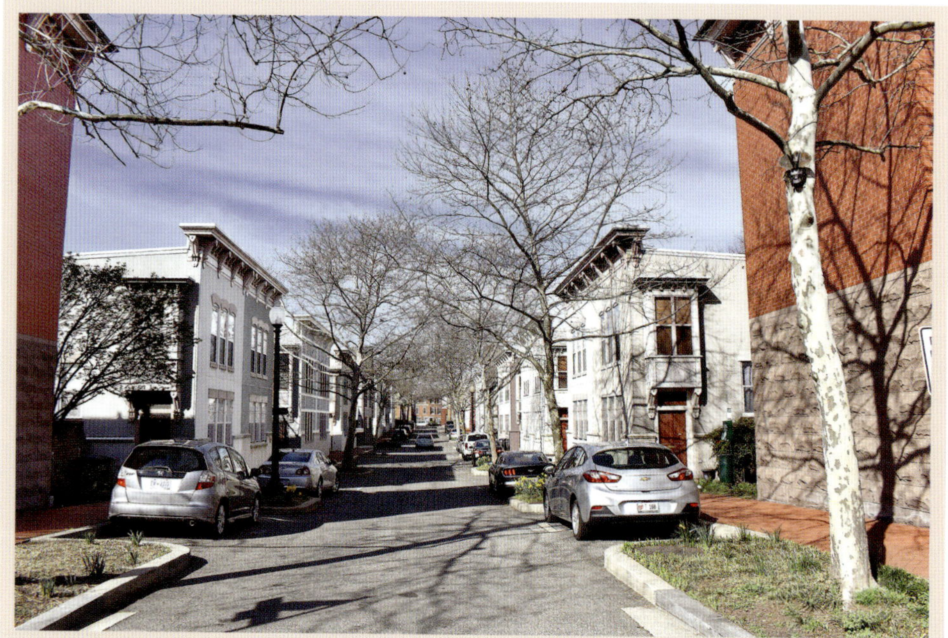

In 1940, Ellen Wilson Homes public housing replaced 70 Navy Place alley dwellings with 215 units for low-income white tenants. The city closed Ellen Wilson Homes in 1988. In 2000, Townhomes on Capitol Hill, a limited equity cooperative, replaced the public housing with the same number of units, building 12 row house types and four duplex types, and adding two new streets. (Photograph by John P. Wymer; courtesy Historical Society of Washington, DC, WY-1558.)

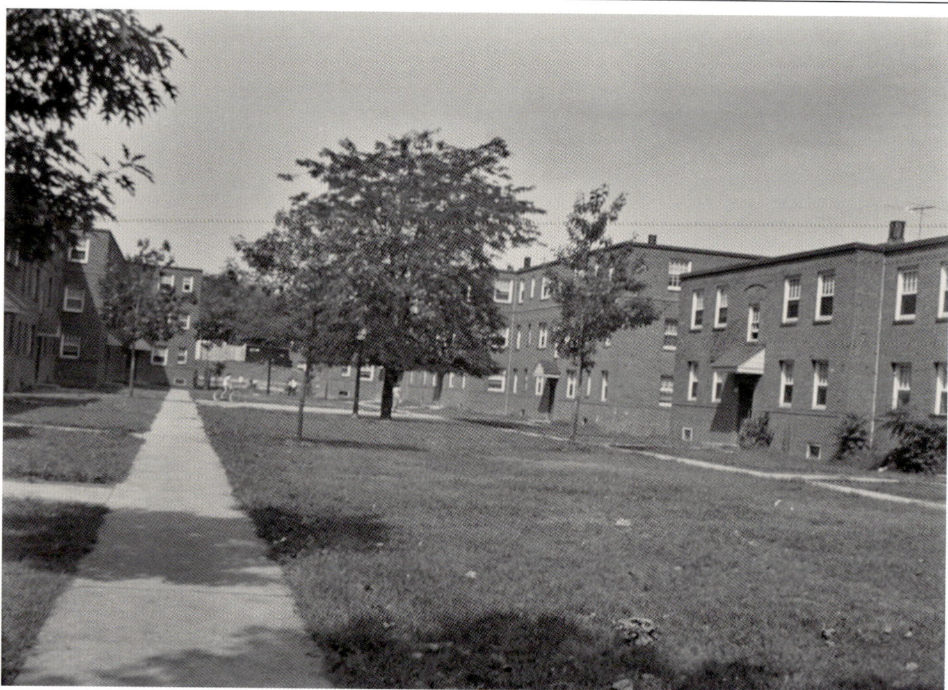

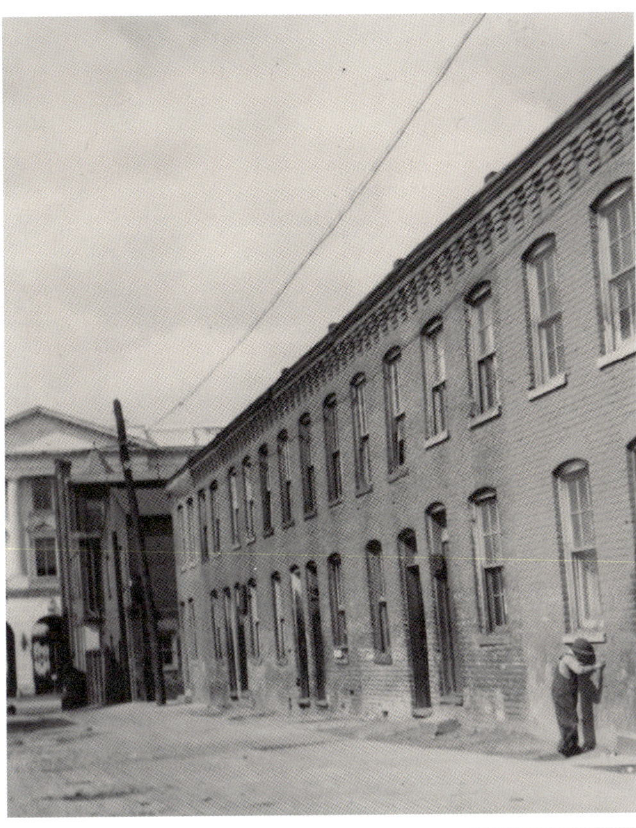

As of 1909, Schott's Alley, located in Square 725 (First Street/Second Street/Constitution Avenue/C Street NE), was home to 172 African Americans and 50 whites. The Russell Senate Office Building is visible in the distance of the past photograph. In 1974, the Hart Senate Office Building replaced almost all the remaining buildings in this square. (Courtesy Historical Society of Washington, DC, HIC-017.)

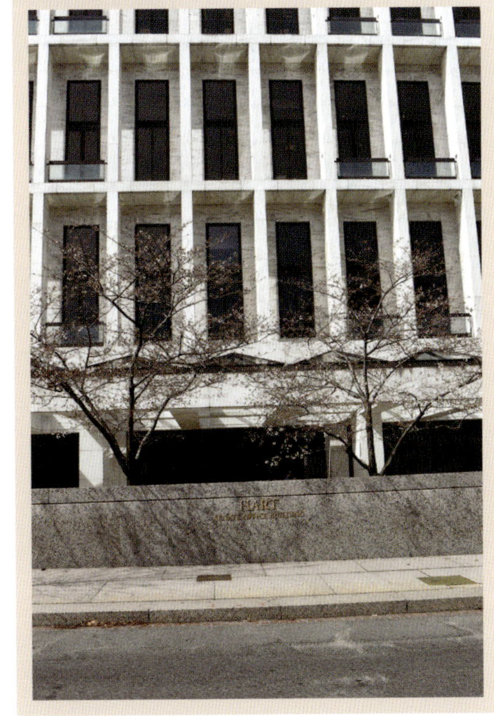

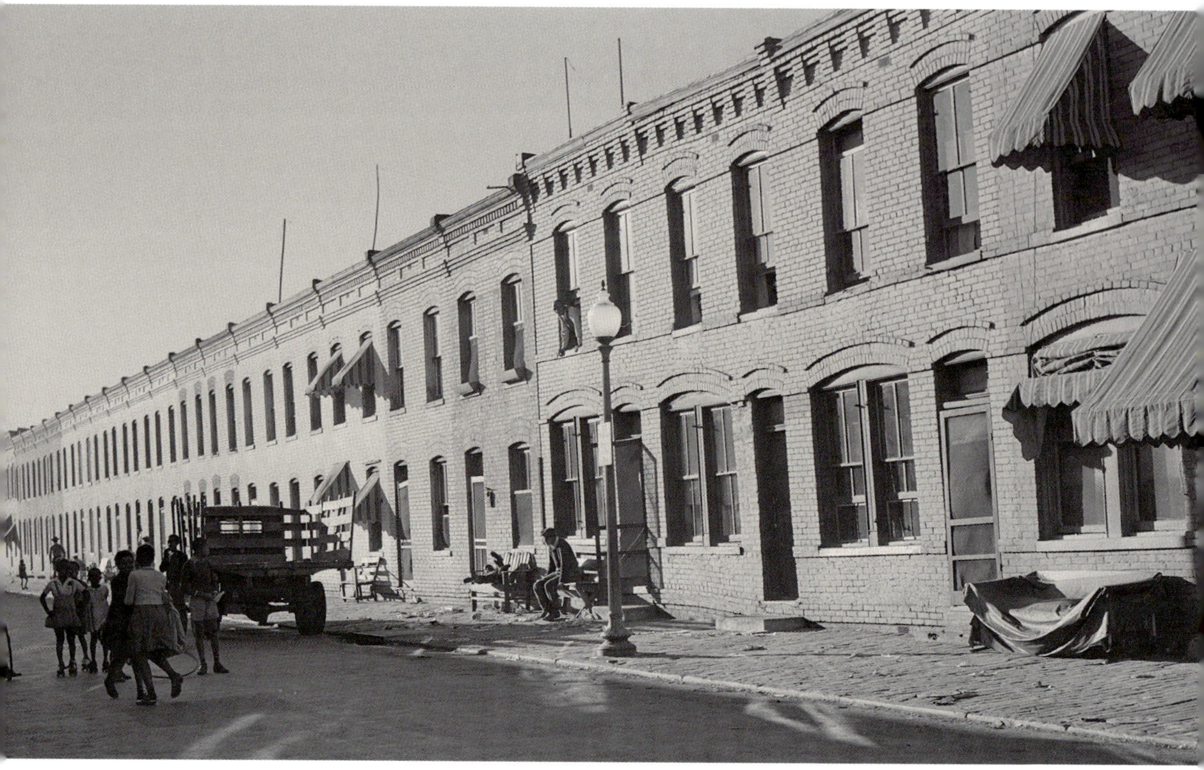

Fenton Place NE, a one-block street in Square 674 (North Capitol/First/K/L Streets NE), was laid out beginning in the 1880s and had approximately 100 brick dwellings. In 1941, when the photograph was taken, residents were primarily African Americans who rented and worked in unskilled or semiskilled jobs. Fenton Place offered two groceries and a deli. The street closed in 1964, replaced by commercial buildings. (Photograph by Marion Post Wolcott; courtesy LOC, LC-USF34-059994-D.)

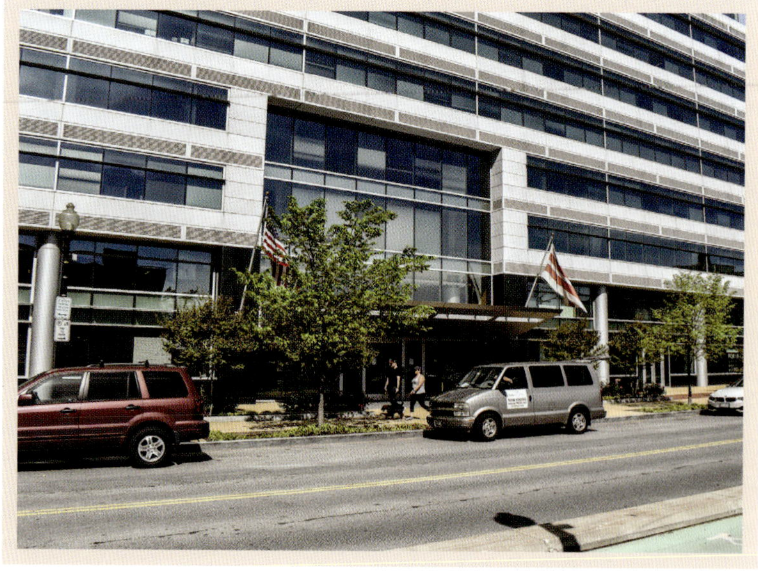

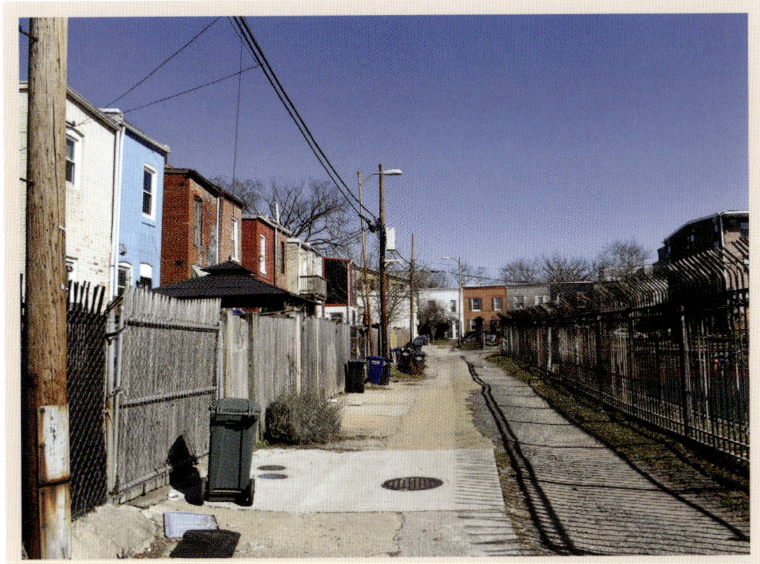

The alley dwellings in London Court SE (also known as Hopkins Place), seen in 1935, were built in Square 1023 (Eleventh/Thirteenth/K/L Streets SE). The National Capital Housing Authority demolished them in 1964, replacing them with Hopkins House public housing (158 units in three- and five-story buildings). (Courtesy Historical Society of Washington, DC, CHS-06842.)

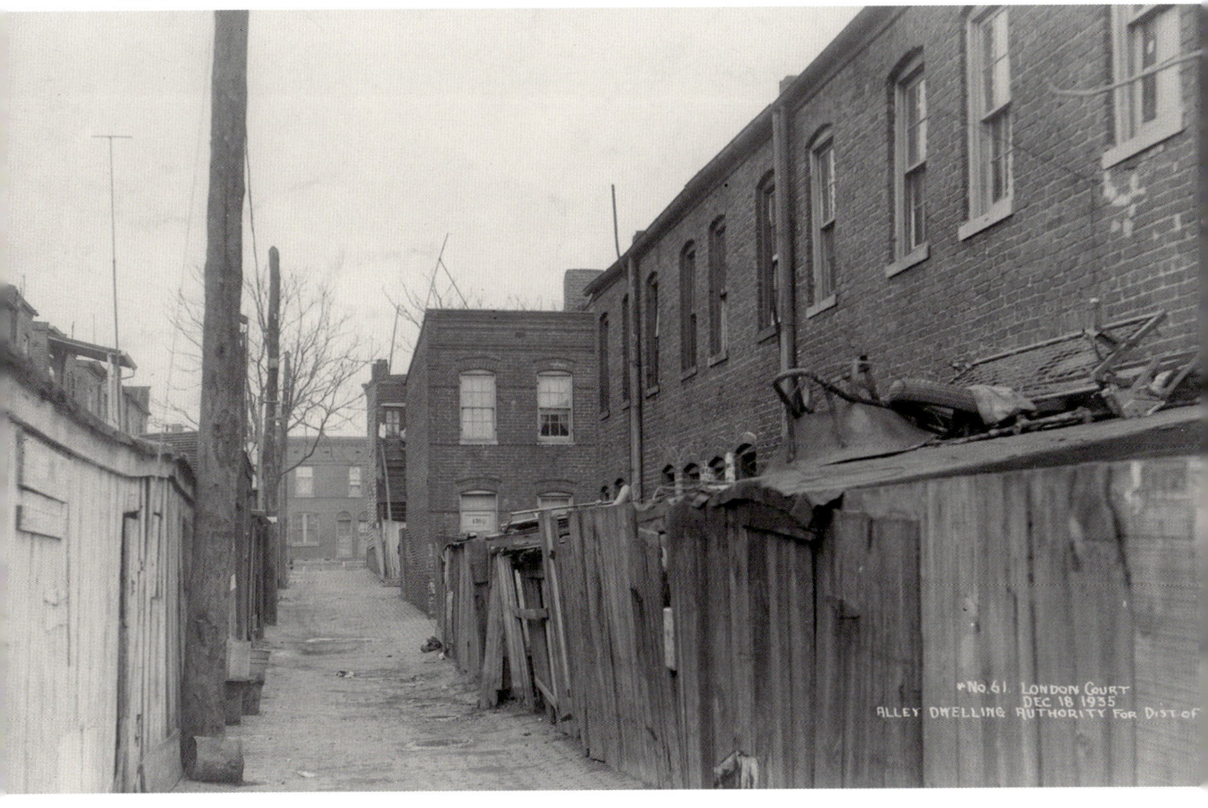

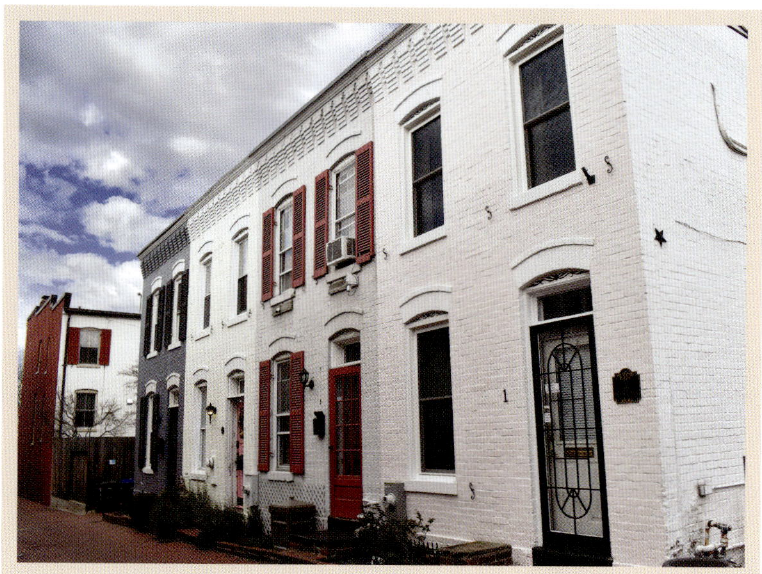

The Terrace Court dwellings near 217 A Street NE were built as rentals in 1889. By 1946, people began to renovate them to live in. They selected green shutters and white walls (the same as George Washington's Mount Vernon) with coach lanterns. They successfully lobbied to make alley dwellings legal. People continue to live in Terrace Court, modifying the 1940s color scheme in some cases. (Courtesy Historical Society of Washington, DC, CPG C112.)

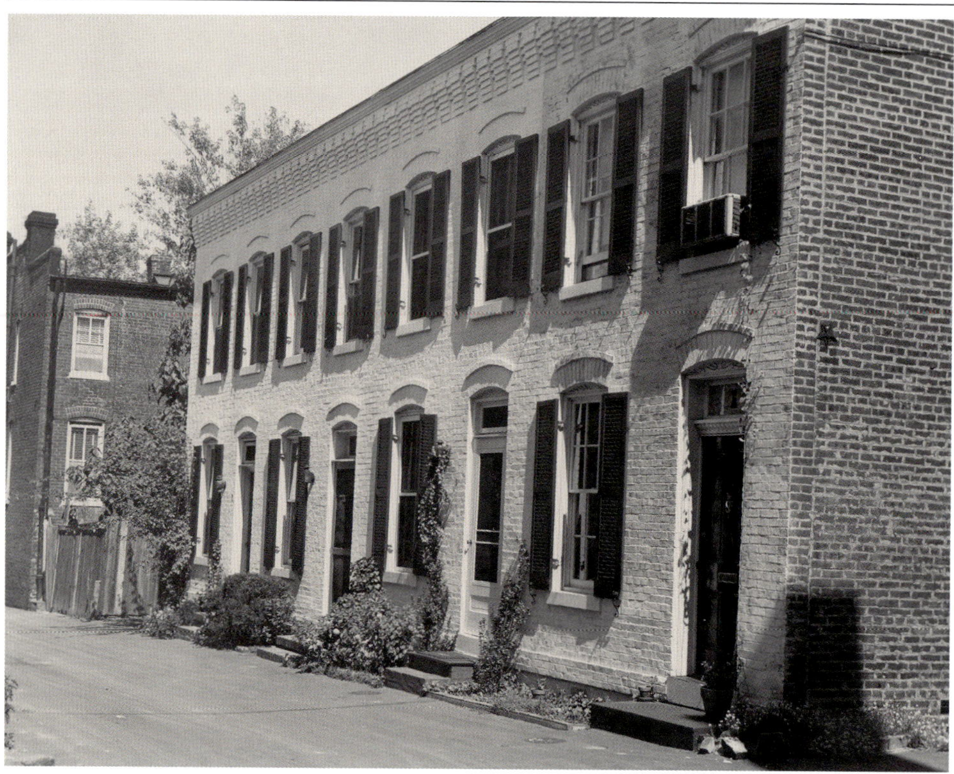

CHAPTER 7

Wind, Fire, and Survivors

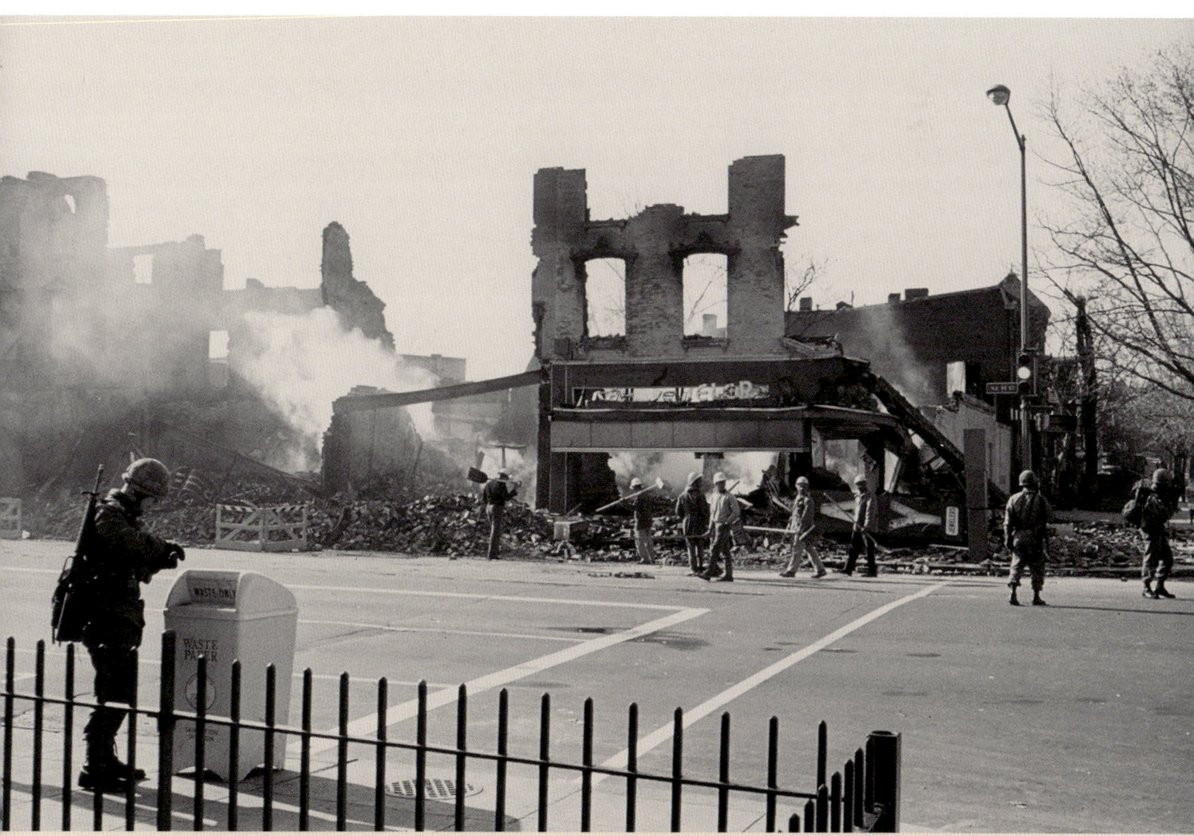

The riots in 1968 following the death of Dr. Martin Luther King Jr. devastated H Street NE. Kay Jewelers, seen here at 801 H Street NE, was burned. Its sign is visible on the ground behind the soldiers. The store did not reopen, and the building was replaced. (Photograph by Emil A. Press; courtesy Historical Society of Washington, DC, PR-1522A.)

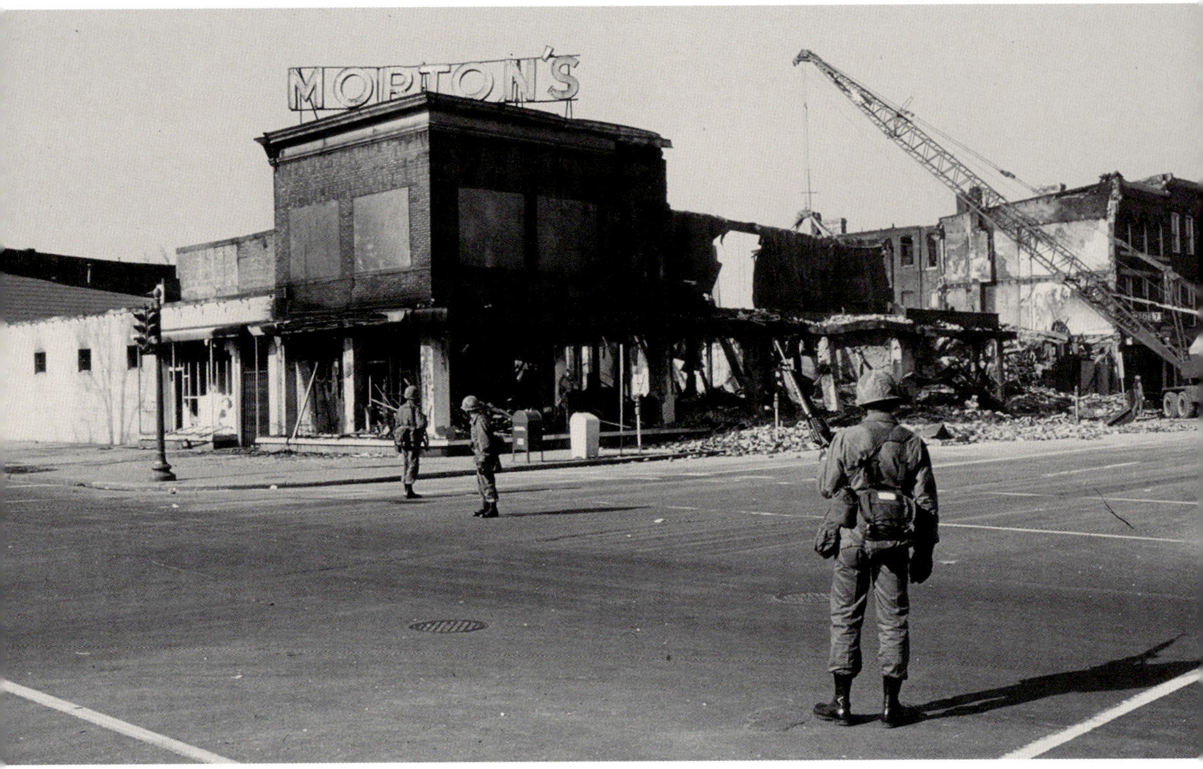

Morton's, a clothing store at 649 H Street NE, and the adjacent businesses, Madera Liquor Store and P&B Valet, burned during the riots in 1968. A new corner building, 645 H Street NE, was constructed in 1987, and as of 2020 was occupied by the Department of Human Services' Economic Security Administration's H Street Service Center. (Photograph by Emil A. Press; courtesy Historical Society of Washington, DC, PR-1522B.)

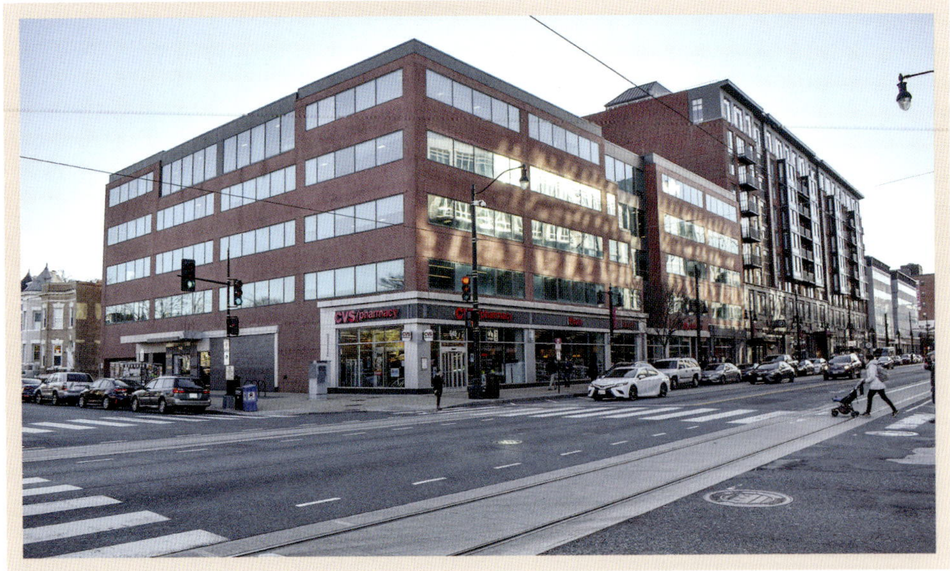

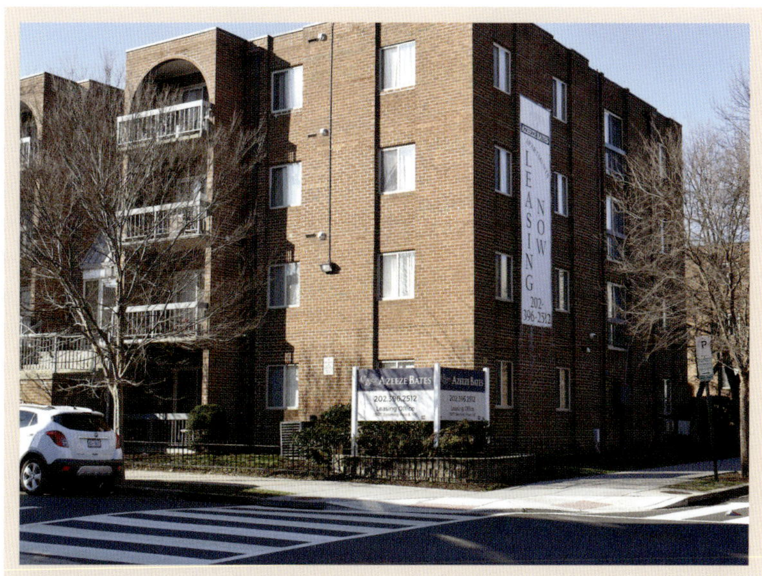

In 1927, Romulus C. Archer Jr., a well-known African American architect, designed the American Ice Company building at 1515 F Street NE, shown in 1949. The company sold refrigerators, "the modern way with ice." The building burned during the 1968 riots. The Acme Supermarket at 1531 F Street NE had the script logo used in the 1950s. In 1980, Horning Bros. built the Azeeze Bates apartments on the site. (Photograph by John P. Wymer; courtesy Historical Society of Washington, DC, WY-1303.)

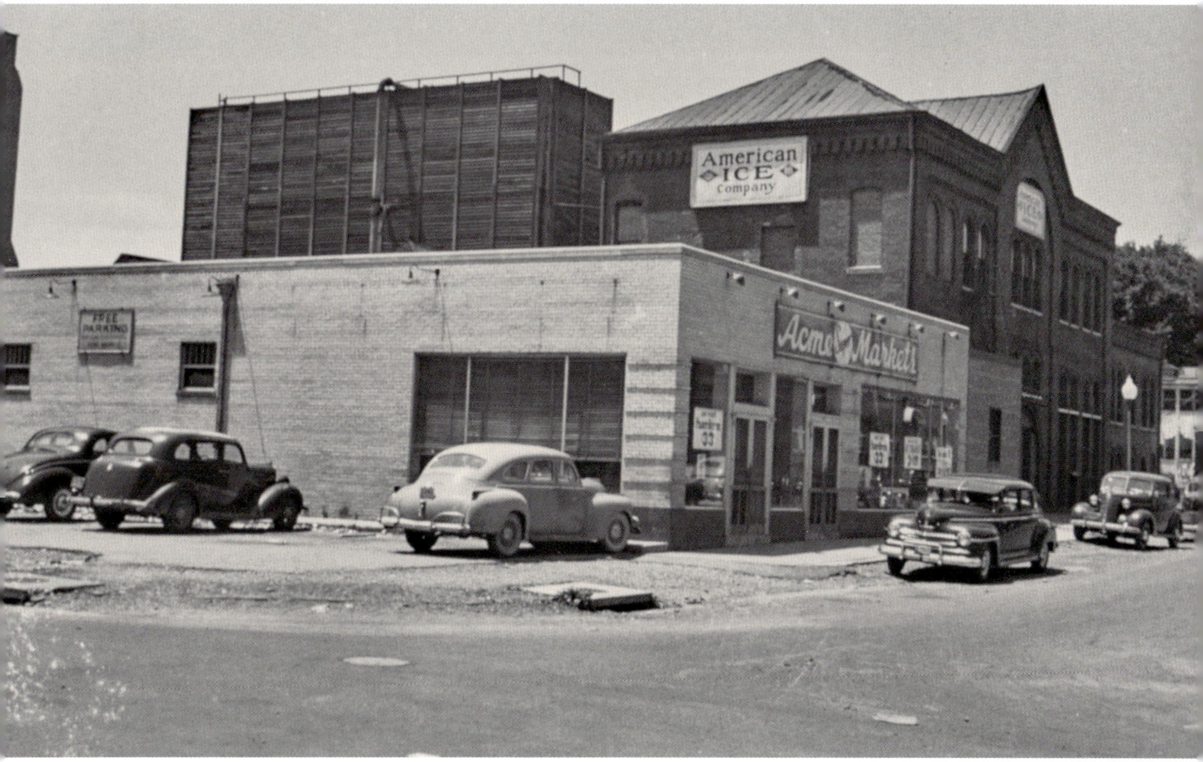

The house at 1525 E Street SE, built in 1879, burned in 1995. After the DC government failed to secure the now-vacant house despite repeated requests, neighbors staged a protest, the "Crack House and Alley Tour," on December 19, 1998. The press release promised visits to urban hellholes, and Kevlar vests were optional. Souvenir T-shirts sold out. The *Washington Post* and the *Washington Times* covered the tour. In 2015, Connell & Schmidt restored the house. (Photograph by author.)

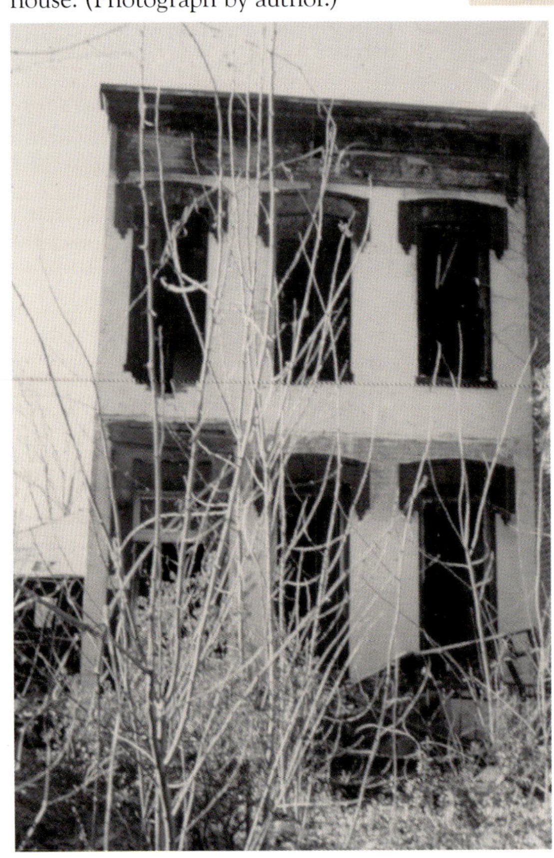

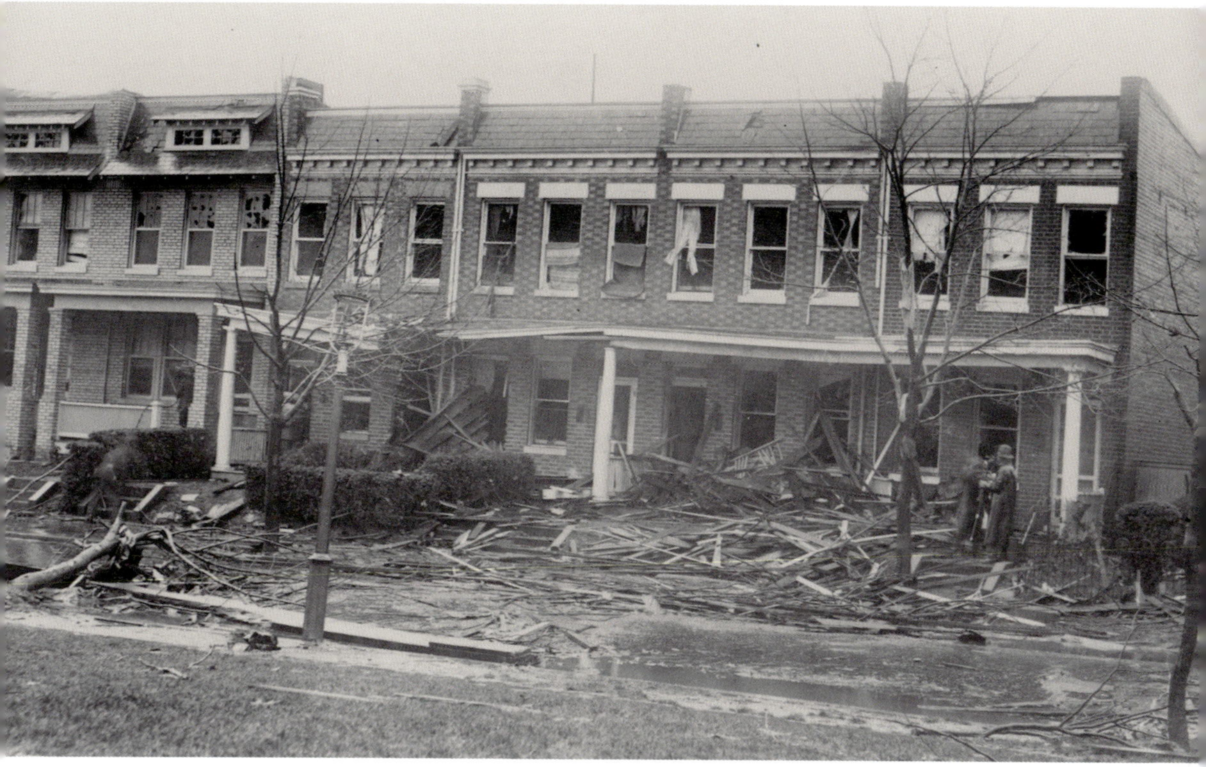

On November 17, 1927, an F2 tornado with winds of 125 miles per hour moved through Capitol Hill, damaging the row houses at 1216–1226 C Street SE. 1216 and 1218 C Street (on the left) were new, completed in 1926 by Herman R. Howenstein. In 1913, Harry A. Kite built the row houses on the right, 1220–1226 C Street. The porches on Kite's houses were not restored. The houses were repaired and remain occupied. (Courtesy LOC, LOT 12354-2.)

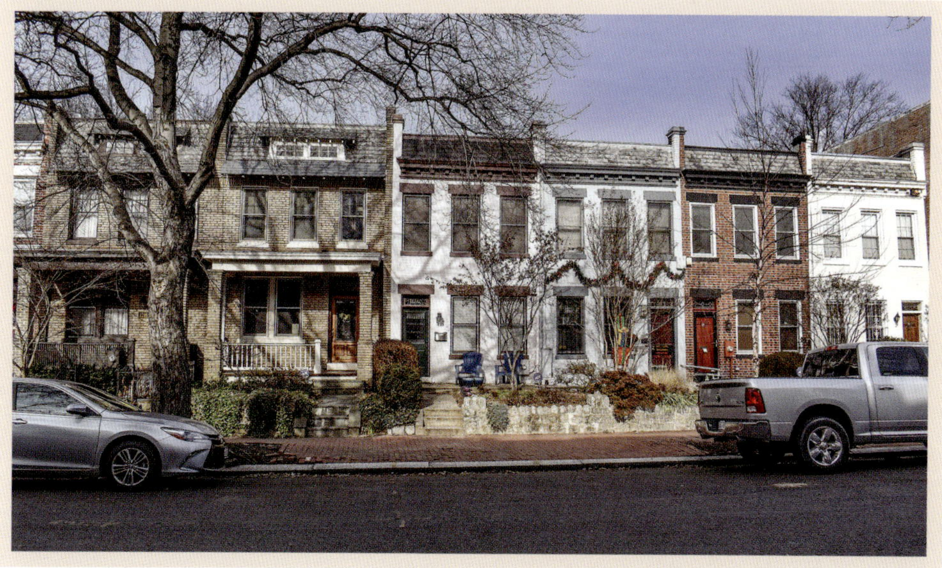

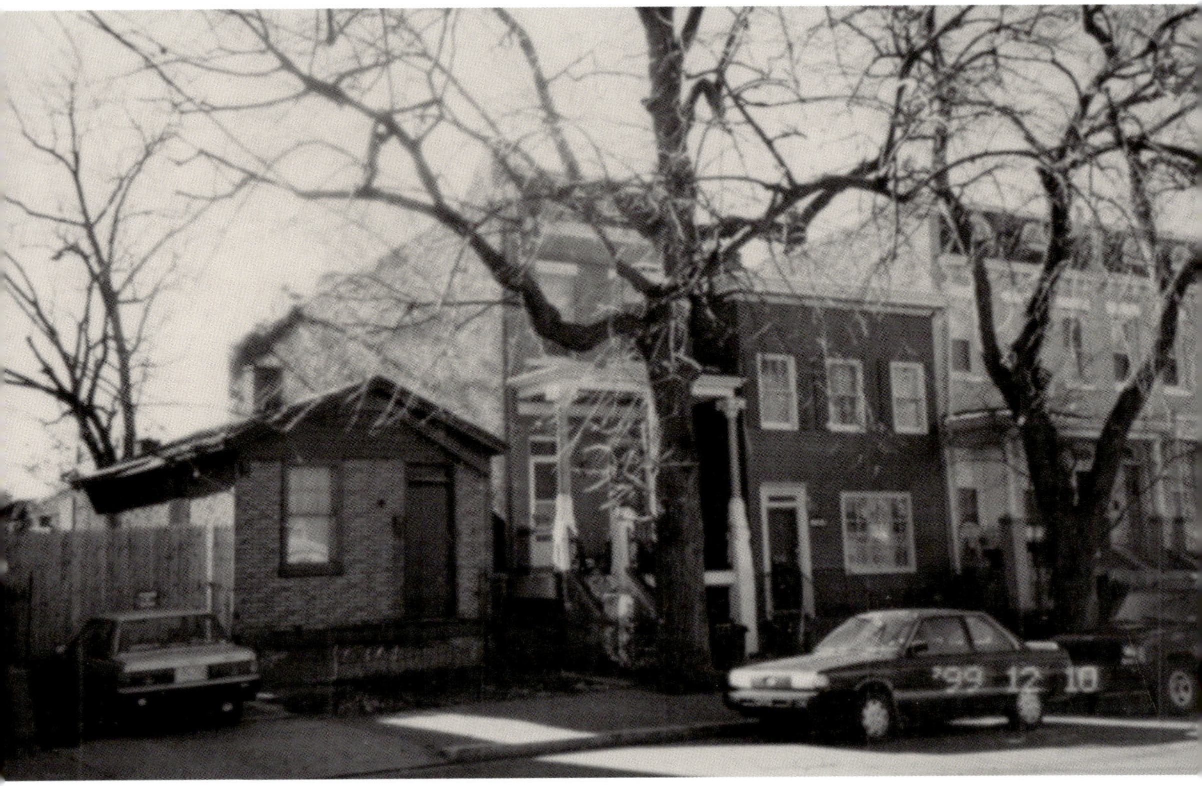

In 1853, John Biegler built this frame shotgun-style house at 1229 E Street SE, a vernacular house with a gable roof, one room wide, and no hallway. By 1999 (past photograph), the house had deteriorated and was covered with asphalt siding and was missing its porch columns. In 2014, the Historic Preservation Review Board allowed it to be moved to the west and reconstructed, reusing as many historic materials as possible. Its restoration was completed in 2019. (Courtesy Nancy Metzger.)

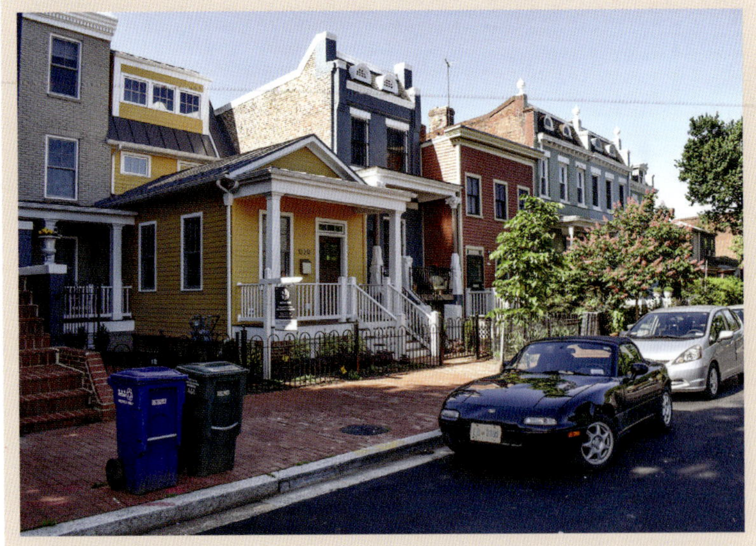

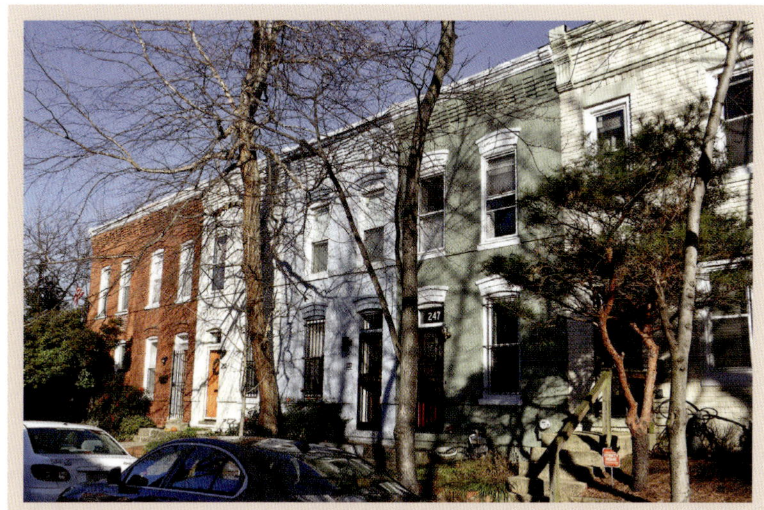

In 1911, A.F. Wood designed and built the five brick row houses on the left, 247–255 Warren Street NE. These modest flat-front houses, intended for the rental market, have brick detailing, corbelled cornices, and segmented arches over the doors and windows, and were not painted. No. 245 was built by Herman R. Howenstein in 1907. Charles Gessford's 1886 one-story brick houses (demolished after 1920) are on the left in the past photograph. (Courtesy LOC, LC-F82-5551.)

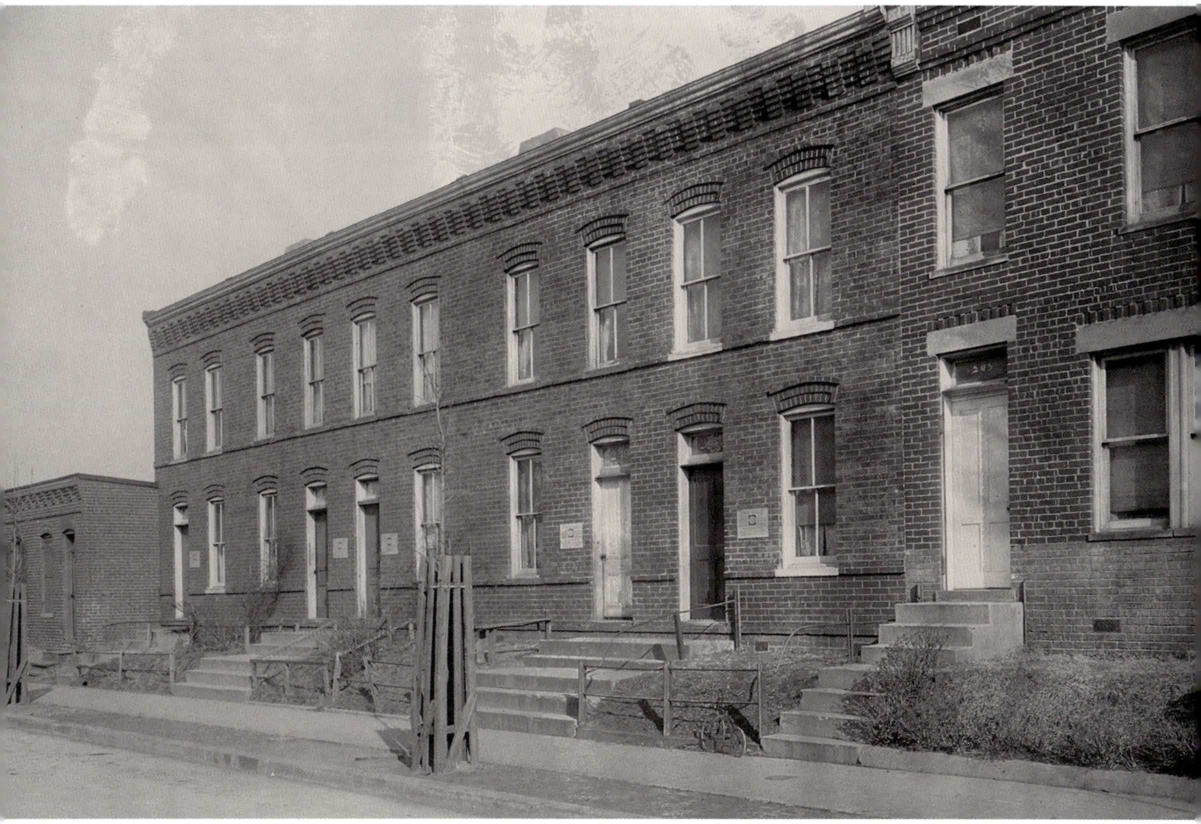

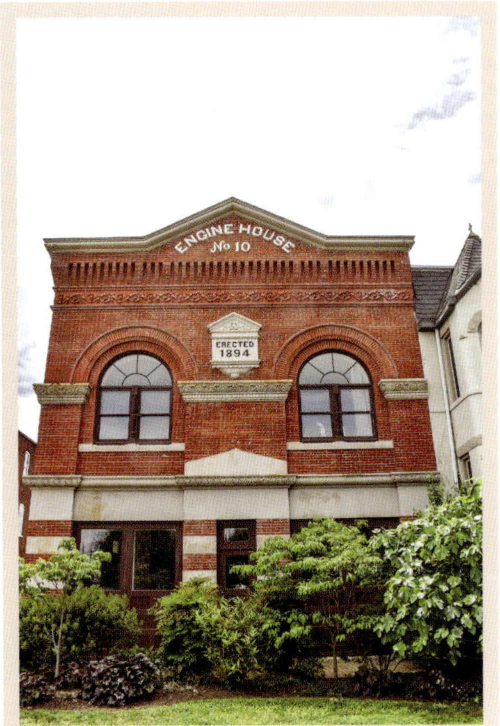

This firehouse at 1341 Maryland Avenue NE, built in 1894, is one of several designed by the well-known architect Leon E. Dessez (1858–1918). His best-known building is the Admiralty House at the Naval Observatory (1893). This firehouse is in the Queen Anne style in pressed brick with deep corbelling and has pilasters capped with stone carvings of acanthus leaves and round arched windows. It is now a private residence. (Courtesy LOC, HABS DC, WASH-160.)

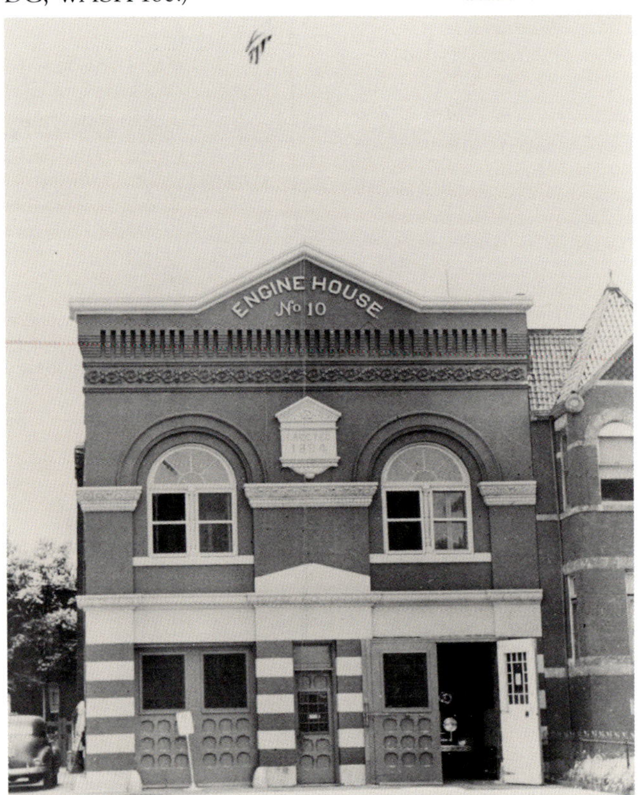

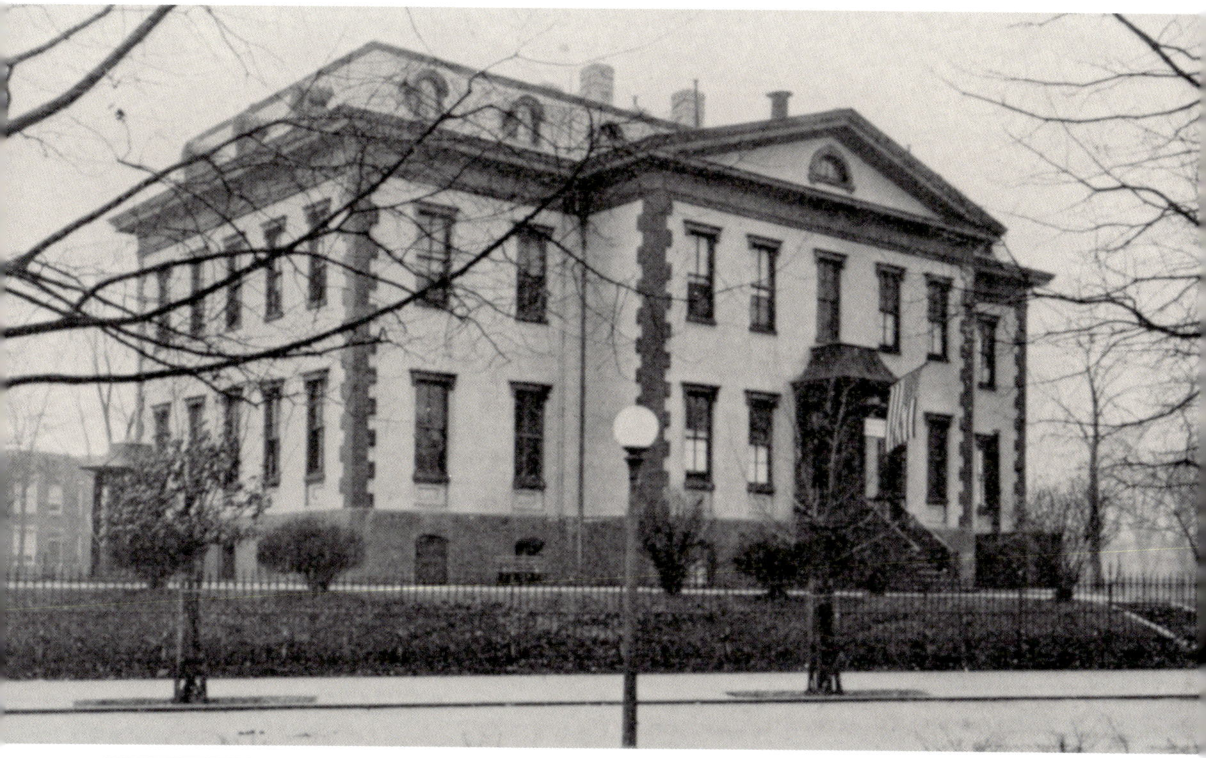

The Old Naval Hospital at 921 Pennsylvania Avenue SE, seen in 1917, was built in 1866 to care for injured sailors and housed various military functions until 1963, when DC government received administrative jurisdiction. By 1998, the building was in poor condition. After extensive community discussion, the Old Naval Hospital Foundation rehabilitated the building as the Hill Center, a space for education, culture, art, music, and community gatherings. (Courtesy Historical Society of Washington, DC, CHS-01182.)

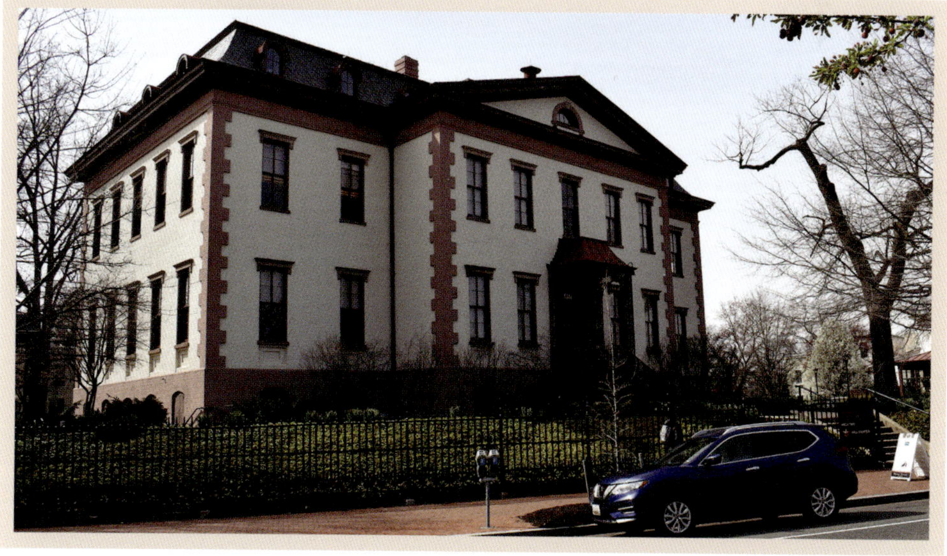

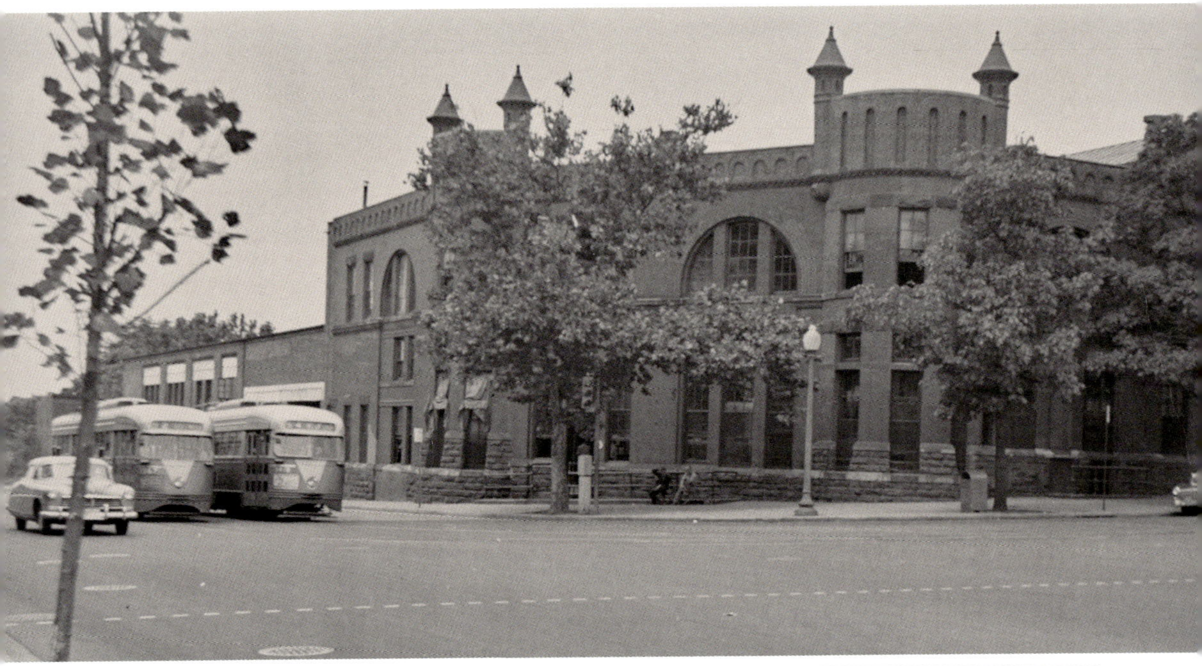

In 1891, the Washington & Georgetown Railroad Company built a streetcar barn (the Navy Yard Carbarn) at 770 M Street SE to serve its line running from Georgetown along Pennsylvania Avenue to Eighth Street SE. At some point after this 1949 photograph was taken, the stone building was painted, so it is also known as the "Blue Castle." (Photograph by John P. Wymer; courtesy Historical Society of Washington, DC, WY-1510.)

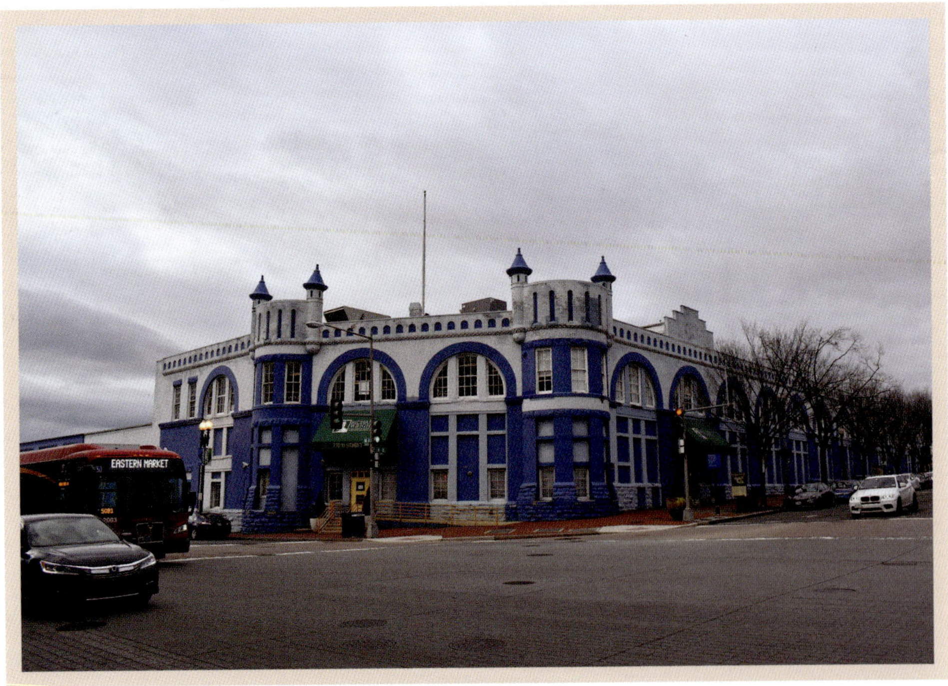

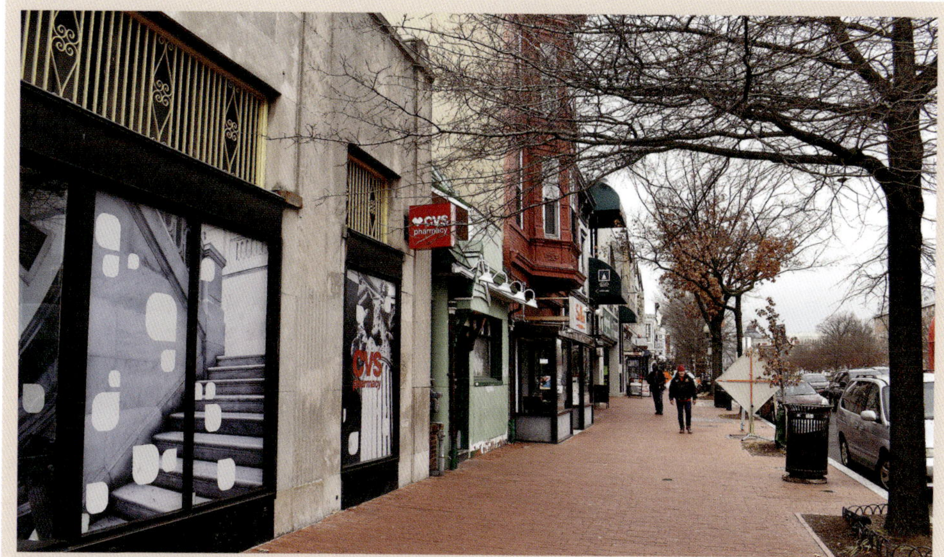

This 1949 photograph shows a soda jerk cleaning the windows at Peoples Drug Store (now CVS) at 661 Pennsylvania Avenue SE. To the right is Little Tavern, a hamburger restaurant/carryout, which opened in 1937 and is now closed. The chain operated many locations in the Baltimore-Washington area. Its motto was "Buy 'Em by the Bag." The last restaurant closed in 2008. (Photograph by John P. Wymer; courtesy Historical Society of Washington, DC, WY-1516.)

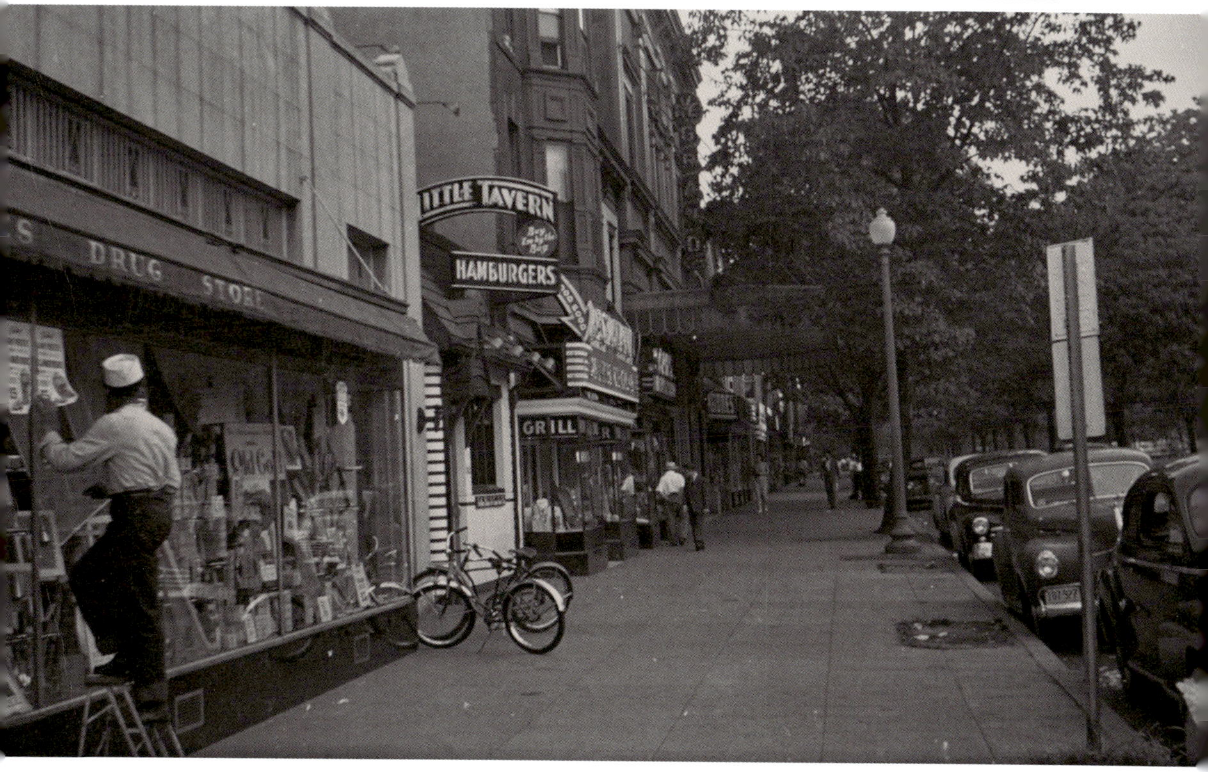

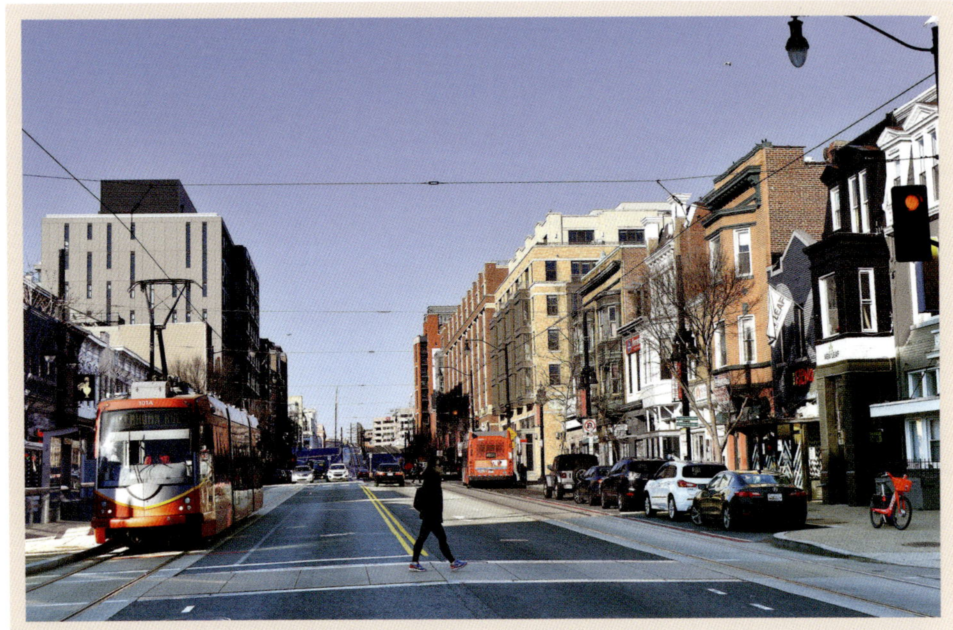

Streetcar service began in 1862 and ended by 1962. The past photograph, taken in 1949, shows men removing streetcar tracks on the 400 block of H Street NE. Streetcars were reintroduced on H Street in 2016. The present photograph shows an eastbound streetcar headed for Oklahoma Avenue NE. (Photograph by Robert S. Crockett; courtesy Historical Society of Washington, DC, CR-107.)

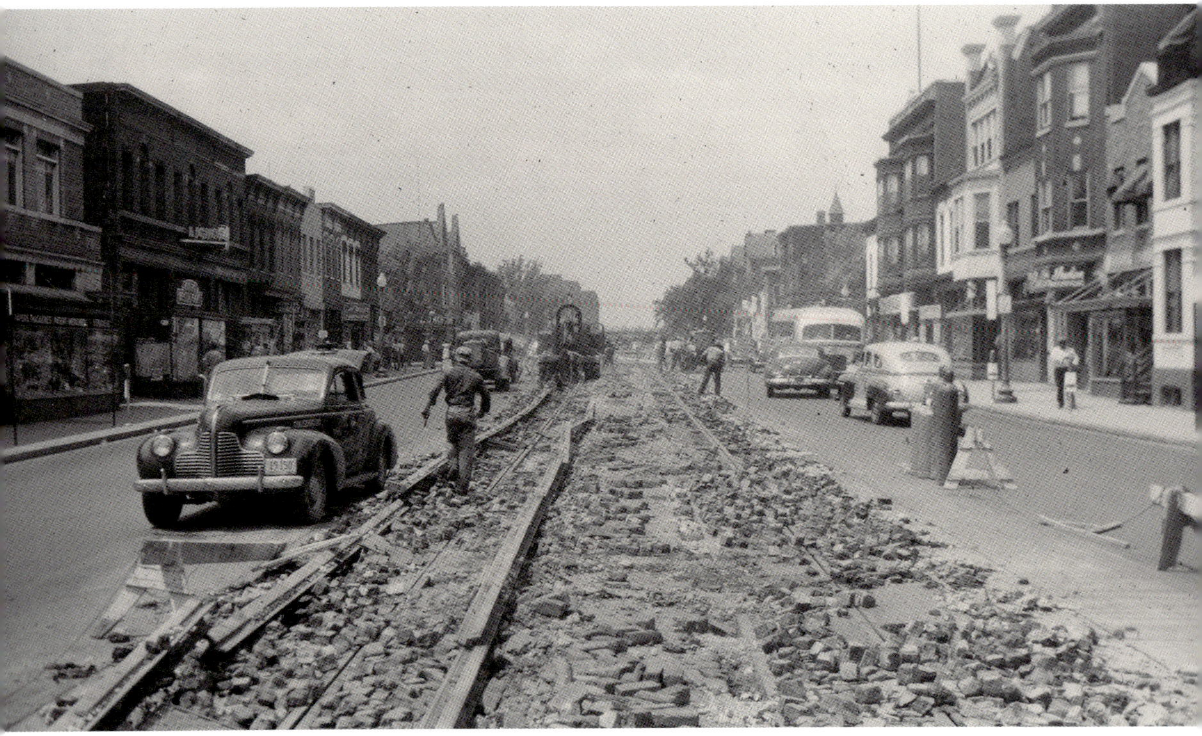

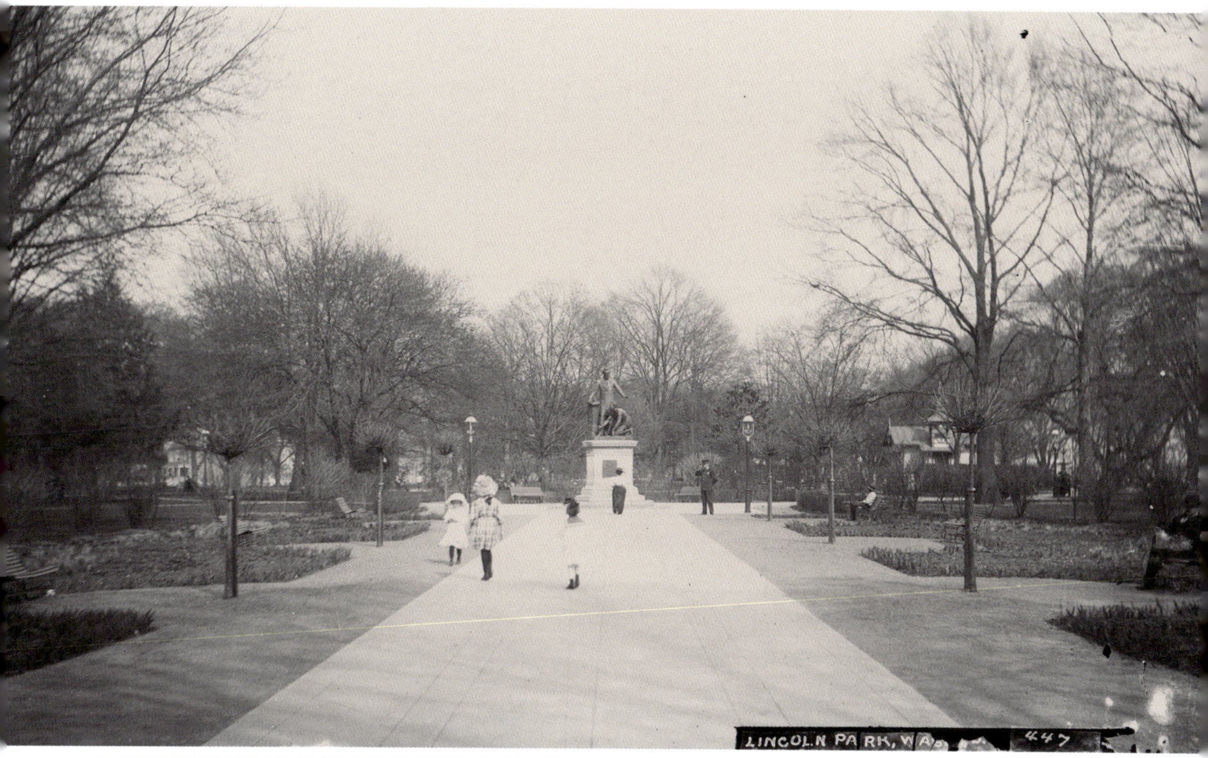

Lincoln Park (Eleventh/Thirteenth/East Capitol Streets) appears in the L'Enfant Plan. A hospital here cared for Union soldiers during the Civil War, and in 1867, the square was named Lincoln Square. The Emancipation Monument, dedicated in 1874, faced west until 1974, when it was rotated to face the Mary McLeod Bethune monument. The Emancipation Monument appears in this 1912 photograph facing west. In the present photograph, looking east, people continue to enjoy the park. (Courtesy Historical Society of Washington, DC, CHS-10129.)

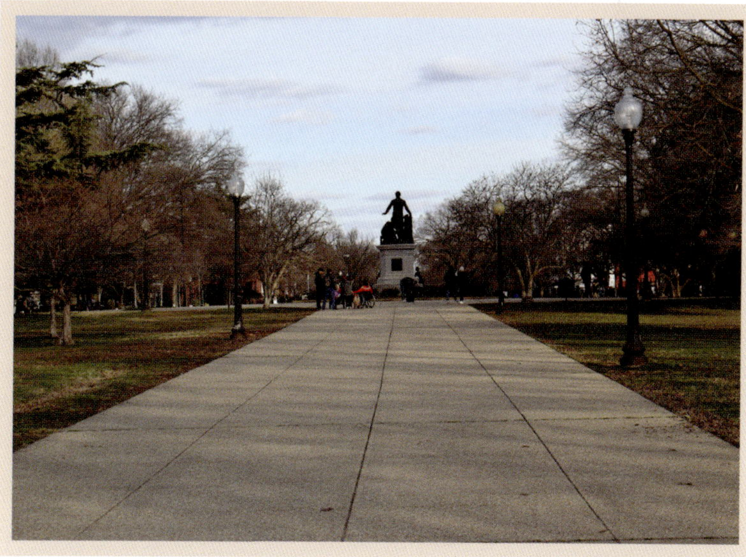

Bibliography

Arnebeck, Bob. *Through a Fiery Trial: Building Washington 1790–1800*. Lanham, MD: Madison Books, 1991.

Asch, Chris Myers, and George Derek Musgrove. *Chocolate City: A History of Race and Democracy in the Nation's Capital*. Chapel Hill, NC: University of North Carolina Press, 2017.

Borchert, James. *Alley Life in Washington*. Chicago, IL: University of Illinois Press, 1982.

DC Department of Transportation. *11th Street Bridges: Final Environmental Impact Statement*. 2007. comp.ddot.dc.gov/Documents.

DC Historic Preservation Office. *DC Historic Alley Buildings Survey*. 2014. planning.dc.gov/

Gilbert, Ben W. *Ten Blocks from the White House: Anatomy of the Washington Riots of 1968*. New York, NY: Frederick A. Praeger, 1968.

Green, Constance McLaughlin. *Washington: A History of the Capital: 1800–1950*. Princeton, NJ: Princeton University Press, 1962–1963.

Gruis, Edward G., ed. *Capitol Hill Prospectus*. Washington, DC: Capitol Hill Restoration Society, 1967. chrs.org/history-and-preservation/chrs-and-the-founding-of-the-historic-district/.

Gutheim, Frederick, and Antoinette J. Lee. *Worthy of the Nation: Washington, DC, from L'Enfant to the National Capital Planning Commission*. Washington, DC: Smithsonian Institution Press, 1977.

Headley, Robert K., and Pat Padua. *Historic Movie Theaters of Washington, DC*. Charleston, SC: Arcadia Publishing, 2018.

Jakle, John A., and Keith A. Sculle. *The Gas Station in America*. Baltimore, MD: Johns Hopkins University Press, 1994.

Langdon, Philip. *Orange Roofs, Golden Arches: The Architecture of American Chain Restaurants*. New York, NY: Knopf, 1986.

Melder, Keith, ed. *City of Magnificent Intentions*. Washington, DC: Intac Inc., 1997.

Peck, Garrett. *Capital Beer*. Charleston, SC: The History Press, 2014.

Scott, Pamela, Charles Carroll Carter, and William C. DiGiacomantonio. *Creating Capitol Hill: Place, Proprietors, and People*. Washington, DC: US Capitol Historical Society, 2018.

Venturi, Robert, Denise Scott Brown, and Steven Izenour. *Learning from Las Vegas*. Cambridge, MA: MIT Press, 1972.

Index

Consistent with our mission to preserve history on a local level, this book was printed in South Carolina on American-made paper and manufactured entirely in the United States. Products carrying the accredited Forest Stewardship Council (FSC) label are printed on 100 percent FSC-certified paper.

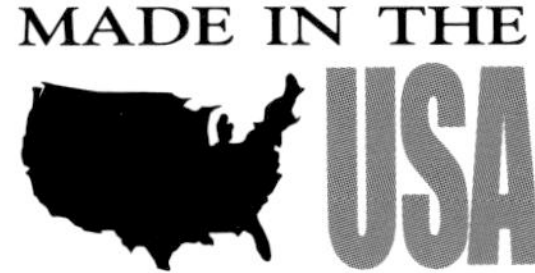